A Model for a Paleoindian Fluted Point Survey

Wm Jack Hranicky RPA
McCary Fluted Point Survey®
Survey Director

authorHOUSE

AuthorHouse™
1663 Liberty Drive
Bloomington, IN 47403
www.authorhouse.com
Phone: 833-262-8899

Published by AuthorHouse 08/10/2021

ISBN: 978-1-4208-4032-2 (sc)

Print information available on the last page.

Any people depicted in stock imagery provided by Getty Images are models, and such images are being used for illustrative purposes only. Certain stock imagery © Getty Images.

This book is printed on acid-free paper.

Contents

Preface

This publication provides an outline for setting up a state-wide Paleoindian fluted point survey. As it is based on the oldest fluted point survey in the U.S., namely the McCary Fluted Point Survey® in Virginia, it offers real-time experiences, methods, procedures, and practices for a survey operation. Any or all parts of this publication may be used freely, just cite the McCary Survey.

Wm Jack Hranicky

Lock and Peters (1996) provide the following on tools:

"Tools constitute the most abundant evidence of hominid behavior over the last two million years. While they have undeniably played an important, if not central, role in hominid ecology, they have also played a role in semiotic behavior. This role probably had its origins in the agonistic use of tools we still see today in non-human primates. When we first encounter extensive use of stone tools, about two million years ago, the ecological context of use is not dramatically different from that of modern apes, and we may assume that the semiotic role of tools was also comparable. By one million years ago tools present patterns well outside the range of anything we know for apes, tempting some scholars to argue for the presence of language. However, given the cognitive and developmental contrasts between tool behavior and language, such conclusions are unwarranted. At 300,000 BP the ecological context of tool behavior was much like that of modern hunting and gathering, but the tools present an enigmatic conservatism in style that suggests a semiotic role very different from that of tools in modern culture. And yet the hominids appear to have had an almost modern intelligence. It is not until relatively late in human evolution, certainly by 15,000, that tools present the volatile time and space patterns typical of the indexical role of modern tools."

McCary Fluted Point Survey®

Photograph of Clovis points taken at an early meeting of the Archeological Society of Virginia (ASV). It is signed by E. B. Sacrey (October 29, 1941), who was the first ASV Secretary. This Folsom/Clovis interest would eventually become the McCary Fluted Point Survey of Virginia.

Ben McCary operated the Survey for approximately 30 years. He turned the Survey over to Michael Johnson and Joyce Pearsall, who operated the Survey during the 1990s. They turned the Survey over to Jack Hranicky, who runs the Survey. The count is 1000+ fluted paleopoints. For a tribute to Ben McCary, see Egloff and McAvoy (1998).

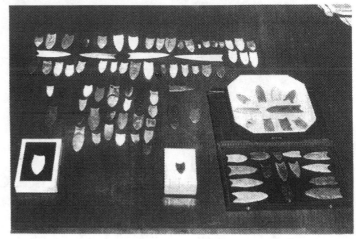

McCary Survey staff are available to go anywhere in the U.S. to advise and assist in setting up a paleopoint survey. This publication may be used freely, but "do" cite the source, if only to commemorate Ben McCary's 30+ years with the Survey. His Survey on fluted points is now the oldest point in the world.

McCary Fluted Point Survey
Webpage: www.mccary-survey.com
Email: hranickyj@va-archaeology
Post Office Box 11256, Alexandria, Virginia 22312

Introduction

In 1982, Louis Brennan compiled a Paleoindian fluted point list for the Eastern States Archeological Federation (ESAF) member societies. It was called the Archaeology of Eastern North America (AENA) Project that compiled 5820 Clovis points for the eastern seaboard. Since this compilation, the number of reported Clovis points has increased been ten-fold, and there is no way to estimate the number of unrecorded fluted points in the so-called *cigar box* of points that

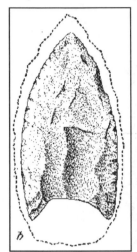

granddad had. With appropriate publicity and selling the idea of recording fluted points for their information, there are still a large number of fluted points to be recorded for archaeology's knowledge base. While the basic definition of a fluted (Clovis) point differs among archaeologists, the classic one is Wormington (1957), which states that the Clovis point is:

> *Fluted lanceolate points with parallel or slightly convex sides and concave bases. They range in length from one and a half to five inches but are usually some three inches or more in length and fairly heavy. The flutes sometimes extend almost the full length of the point but usually they extend no more than half way from the base to the tip. Normally, one face will have a longer flute than the other. The fluting was generally produced by the removal of multiple flakes. In most instances the edges of the basal portion show evidence of smoothing by grinding. Certain fluted points found in the eastern United States resemble the Clovis type, but they have a constriction at the base which produces a fish-tailed effect. These have sometimes been called Ohio points or Cumberland points. Many of these tend to be somewhat narrower relative to their length than other fluted points.* The earliest published Clovis (see drawing b) point in Virginia is Holmes (1897).

Surveys have, if only for this reason, proven that Clovis technology originated in the Southeast and that Mason's (1962) paper argument was correct:

> *... fluted points of every description except Folsom are far more numerous in the East, particularly in the Southeastern United States ... and this area has produced the greatest diversification in fluted point styles.*

Brennan's AENA Project set forth to prove Mason's eastern argument and, in doing so, clearly amplified the need to record Clovis points on a state-by-state basis. He does note: *The fluted point is, at the moment, without a parent.*[1] This model for a survey is a continuation of the AENA Project's basic goal – recording Clovis points. And, each paleopoint has physical properties that form the point's topography which is also called morphology.

Publication Objectives

This publication provides an overview of how to set up a fluted point survey. It provides all processes, procedures, and practices for a survey which are based on the McCary Fluted Point Survey® of Virginia. Additionally, it provides an overview of using survey data for archaeological modeling and simulations. Survey data validity, validation, and storage/organization methods are also discussed. Basic recording concepts and ethics are presented throughout the publication.

---

[1] Virginia's Cactus Hill site has proven that the Clovis technology was not the ground-floor for stone toolmakers in the Americas.

This publication is divided into:

- **Part One – Basic Survey Operations** – applies to the basic set up and operations of a paleopoint survey.

- **Part Two – Basic Modeling for Surveys** – applies to the basic methods in modeling as they would apply to a survey.

The Original McCary Survey Publication
ASV Quarterly Bulletin Volume 2, Number 1, 1947

Part One – Basic Survey Operations

Clovis and Its Kin

Clovis is used here as a generalized term for all Paleoindian fluted, and in some cases, nonfluted, lanceolate projectile points. This time period contains numerous varieties of the lanceolate form. As with the McCary Fluted Point Survey ® of Virginia, the term generally means fluted lanceolate points that were made during the Paleoindian era. Each survey must define its meaning and use of the Clovis type. Each paleopoint is unique and represents membership in an archaeological class and/or type. And, each point has physical properties that form its topography, which is also called the point's morphology.

The Point Survey

In 1947, Ben C. McCary[2] started the Virginia Folsom (became Clovis, then fluted) point survey.[3] This survey has become the oldest paleopoint survey in the U.S. It is the basis for this publication and has served as a model for numerous states' surveys. With nearly 60 years of recording points, the Survey's hands-on experiences and recommendations make up this publication.

A point survey is an excellent example of archaeology without artifacts in that archaeology is a science for the accumulation of data and producing knowledge, not a science for the accumulation of artifacts. Naturally, artifacts and all their masses are part of archaeology – the evidences of the past, but their purpose is to produce a history about the antiquity of humans and their lifeways. Artifacts are historical entities and are physical forms of human-driven events of ancestral cultures. A fluted point survey simply records data from a specialized resource from prehistory. These data are then translated, reconfigured, compiled, etc. into chronological sequences of human events. Artifacts loan their physical presence to the survey for recordation, then go home to whomever owns them. A survey is then not a short-term curation process for these specimens; it is a long-term curation for the data that these artifacts contain. A survey contributes to the philosophy for knowledge in the study of antiquities.

While use and operation of a fluted point survey vary nationally, a survey's justification generally includes an archaeological perspective of:

- Tracing cultural resources
- Acquisition of site locations
- Collecting archaeological data
- Monitoring resource transfers
- Populating state distribution maps
- Providing point residue analysis
- Recording point recovery locations
- Verifying classification schema
- Identifying point concentrations
- Single point resource for public reporting

---

[2] For a tribute to Ben C. McCary, see Egloff and McAvoy (1998).
[3] Back in the 1940s, McCary was influenced by two publications: Roberts' (1938) The Folsom Problem in American Archaeology and Howard's (1943) Evidence of Early Man in North America. Additionally, he did extensive work at the Williamson site in Dinwiddie County, Virginia (see summary in: Benthall and McCary 1973).

- And, numerous other factors.

A survey is an information producing enterprise with roots in the old days of Indian artifact collecting (Figure 1). It was, stated simply, bragging rights for counting individual point ownerships within amateur societies. As societies matured, the scientific enterprise became the guidelines, and progress has moved the concept of the survey into what can be called the database of history. Hranicky (2003a) provides an overview and justification for a fluted point survey, but as noted several years ago by Hranicky (1989), there is a tremendous amateur and collector involvement in recording Clovis points. And a survey must recognize and approach the collector and art worlds of antiquity ownerships – or, simply, go where the points are.[4]

A survey is a record-and-publish operation. Private vs. public ownership of antiquities is not a crusading ideology for any survey. As such, it must recognize that the artifact world is divided into collections: those inside and those outside archaeology. And, furthermore, a survey is neither an *artifact traffic cop* to stop illegal looting and selling of artifacts nor an *artifact banker* to set monetary values on points.

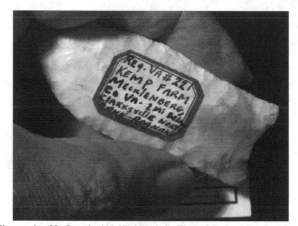

Figure 1 – McCary's (1947) Virginia Fluted Point Number 221.
Label has the same information that was published by the Survey in the
Quarterly Bulletin of the Archeological Society of Virginia.

A survey has its geographical coverage and goes where the artifacts (data) are. Its premier responsibility is: record and publish data on Paleoindian fluted points. As the survey operates within its published guidelines (procedures, standards, policies, and practices), its position in academia, state/federal agencies, various Indian tribes, and the archaeological community should have acceptance and be reality free from various concerns about ownership, trading, and destruction of America's prehistoric antiquities.

Definition of a Paleopoint Survey

A fluted point survey is defined as the scientific process of collecting, recording, and publishing data that were obtained analytically from paleopoints which were made by Early Americans during the Paleoindian era of North America. A survey is an ongoing process of collecting time-stamped data from a point recording session with a point owner; data which may never be updated.

---

[4] For basic point nomenclature, see Appendix I.

Best Practices

Within any survey, there will probably be exceptions to policy, violations to standards, and deviation to procedures; all of which could damage the credibility of the survey. The world of recording fluted points is so vast that recordation will never be perfect. Thus, the suggestion is that a survey, in addition to its policies, develop a "best practices" document or an overall philosophy that operates "kind-a" behind the scene (Table 1) of a survey's public nature. Mistakes may occur, but they are corrected and noted in lessons learned records. Best practices are basically reactionary and rely on experiences of personnel.

Table 1 – Best Practices	
Inventory	Inventory is a catch-all phrase that identifies all cultural resources that pertain to the survey's provenance. The survey maintains knowledge of them; not their control(s). The survey must know its "topic" world.
Change control	Technology is constantly changing as well as methodologies in archaeology. The survey must continually update its polices, procedures, etc.
Technical support	Maintain best available resources, equipment, and talent; regardless of this effort, technical support will never be adequate. The survey must actively recruit the best technical support in and outside archaeology.
Security	Monitor internal and external procedures to points and associated data. Security procedures should be covered in the survey's procedures documents.
Ethics	Probably this will always be mediation among all parties in the study of prehistoric collections, especially their acquisition and disposal. Basically, this is a tip-toe practice.
Data migration	Probably best defined in the survey's procedural scope, but "old" data will haunt the survey's operation. The survey should continually provide notices of new survey releases and publication.
Point ownership	Monitor ownership and make attempts to track points. Once a point is recorded, no assumption should be made about its finality. The survey should try to track paleopoints in its provenance.
Continuous validation	Always continue to validate survey data. Circumstances, methods, and people are constantly changing in the real world: as such, a survey must be diligent in maintaining best practices so that data represent the true artifact world.
Quality control	Always perform expert evaluation on submitted points and submit all point reports for survey committee reviews.
Scientific method	Always use scientific methods and principles.

Nomenclature and Terminology

Standardized nomenclature and terminology are basic requirements for recording and documenting survey points. Nomenclature is, of course, part of the classification process which, by its vocabulary, conveys meaning and results to other archaeological researchers. Hranicky (2004) provides a guide for terminology standards in archaeology.

For example, the term "Clovis" has numerous definitions in the literature; in fact, most archaeologists create their personal definitions when writing research results. For this publication, Clovis is used generically for all Paleoindian points, fluted or unfluted. Hranicky and Johnson (2005) provide photographs and drawings of approximately 1000 McCary Survey points. These points show a wide range of styles, manufacturing methods, lithic materials, and functional uses. When viewing the total paleopoint population, there is Clovis and there is *not* Clovis. Thus, a Clovis absolute definition is never achievable in archaeology, but most paleopoints (a prehistoric entity) have enough attributes and traits to make themselves recognizable; and thus, are classified into archaeological types.

Concepts and Standards

Appendix A provides standards and concepts which are the basis for methods, procedures, policies, and practices used in recording fluted points (as in: Hranicky and Johnson 2005). They are used by the McCary Fluted Point Survey® and provide the basics for its scientific point recording. Appendix B provides procedures that a survey should use, and Appendix C provides survey policies. Obviously, they can be modified for other surveys or point laboratories. For point recording, the following are recommended requirements:

- Established-written standards
- Established-written procedures
- Established-written policies
- Established-written processes.

All of which create an operating system which produces reliable and replicable point data. Basically, all scientific laboratories have rigorous methodologies which are based on years of experiences in becoming *scientific*. Processes, artifact patterns, and interpretations are the subject of these procedures (investigations) and constitute a total technology resource for prehistory. According to Washburn (1953):

The assumption seems to have been that description (whether morphological or metrical), if accurate enough and in sufficient quantity, could solve problems of process, pattern, and interpretation. . . . But all that can be done with the initial descriptive information is to gain a first understanding, a sense of problem, and a preliminary classification. To get further requires an elaboration of theory and method along different lines.

Concepts, standards, and database logic as they apply to archaeology are defined as:

Archeological Concepts – culture, which is often lacking in archaeological presentations (many of which never use the word *Indian*), is the essence of all archaeological research and investigations. Culture is but one of three elements present in all archaeological concepts, namely culture, technology, and chronology. These basic properties are then viewed over space, and when coupled with change analyses, the prehistoric record is presented. Phillips and Willey (1953) discuss the importance of this combination to archaeological theory:

It is impossible to image an artifact type or cultural unit that is not defined with reference to specific forms and does not also have distribution in space and duration in time. However, though invariably present, these three diverse properties may and do vary enormously in proportion one to another ... It becomes essential, therefore, in the definition and use of archeological concepts of whatever nature to understand precisely what quantities of space, time, and formal content are involved in the mixture.

Standards (Needs) – within the lithic technology enterprise (and scientific archaeology in general), standards allow:

1 – Consistent reference material and data
2 – Comparisons among various research activities by outsiders
3 – Precision in data collection and reporting

4 – Prediction based on solid data and their inferences
5 – Consistency in descriptions and definitions
6 – Means for data/artifact verification.

Database Logic – using standard database design for data maintenance. Basics are:

1 – First principle – first-hand observations and recording
2 – Second principle – standard terminology and identification (classification)
3 – Third principle – accurate functional properties and typology.

These principles are discussed below. In addition to the above survey documentation, there are numerous state/federal standards that can be used. The following are excellent sources:

- Curation of Federally-owned and Administered Archaeological Collections (36 CFR 79)
- Cultural Resource Standards – Handbook (New York Archaeological Council, Standards Committee
- Archaeological Curation Standards and Guidelines (North Carolina Department of Cultural Resources)
- Section 106 – National Historic Preservation Act (NHPA).

Basic Modeling

There are many archaeological modeling techniques, and selecting or building a model for paleopoint surveys involves understanding their cultural conditions and technological functions in prehistory. A state-wide survey is an enormous task involving recording, recordkeeping, and reporting point data. This model and publication are based on the operation of the McCary Fluted Point Survey® of Virginia and can be used freely to design, establish, and implement paleopoint surveys in other states.

The principal factors in setting up a fluted point survey are determining membership and chronological range for paleopoints. Questions to be asked: Is it solely Clovis, open to any fluted point, and what standards are applied in determining classification for these categories? Basic references, such as Justice (1989), Perino (1985 and 1991), Hranicky (2003), and Hranicky and Johnson (2005), offer insights for making these determinations, but as suggested, written criteria for standards and acceptance policy offer the best way to ensure database validity and credibility. If the survey is not used for all paleopoints, then classification and nomenclatures should be written and implemented regarding point inclusions. Figure 2 shows basic archaeological relationships for a point in a survey.

While counting numbers of fluted points found in a state may be an interesting pastime, this practice offers little data for the study of Paleoindian technology in the U.S. Most archaeologists would concur that all data be collected from discovered fluted points and maintaining these data for access to all scholars is a high priority in archaeology. However, the type of discovery still causes concern in the professional community. The only argument is: valid data produce valid information. This model offers survey architecture, provides a basic survey operation and implementation, and presents practical factors needed to make a survey work. The survey database should comply to standard industry designs, for example Fleming and von Halle (1989).

Regional and national surveys provide massive amounts of point data. Unless searchable, these data can be overwhelming to researchers. Their major faults lie in finding, updating and validating point data from various point surveys. The ideal location is the state-level institution where access and maintenance can be controlled and monitored by both the amateur and professional archaeological communities, and including qualified collectors. As described below, data collecting requires strict methodologies to ensure that data are valid and trustworthy.

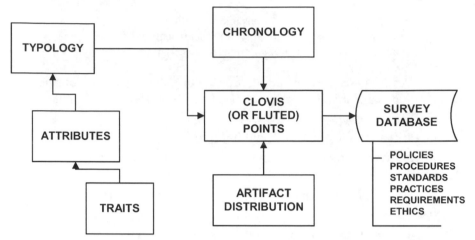

Figure 2 – Establishing Basics for Recording Paleopoints in a Survey

This survey model's focus requires recording data, storing data, and reporting data that are available to anyone who requests survey data for scholarly research. This model does not suggest that a survey become involved in the acquisition and storage of Clovis materials. The survey is intended to present interpretations of its data files or maintain records so as to suggest some type of organization that reflects culture histories. A survey provides data freely to scholars who create their interpretations based on their research philosophies and methods. If available, the survey should make casts of the points that are given survey numbers. Surveys should always photograph points using digital and film techniques.

As presented, a survey should (must) have written policies, practices, and standards in place so that survey operation can be consistent, reliable, and maintainable. The survey is not a short-term activity; thus, plans should be made for staffing, funding, and storing files. As a precaution, surveys are often questioned as to why certain points were included and, of course, why certain points were excluded. Survey operating documents can often answer the question and influence answers for future questions. McCary Survey policies, procedures, and standards are found in Hranicky and Johnson (2005) and can be used freely in organizing and implementing a survey.

A survey must determine its policy should a fake point get into the database. Once a survey point number is issued and published, it is very difficult to correct the mistake. The recommendation is to remove the flake data and leave the point number empty in the database. An explanation is needed. However, removing the record and its number is also a possibility but is a major problem, especially for statistical studies. There is no easy answer for this problem. Survey personnel should – when in the slightest doubt – not record the point.

Basically, archaeological data, namely site-oriented data, are what constitute contemporary archaeology. However, as with the McCary Survey, most artifact data that are collected come from surface finds, and in far too many cases, artifacts are hand-me downs that do not have specific provenances. Most survey databases when viewed collectively (nation-wide) are enormous resources which are largely ungoverned, are somewhat credible, and are difficult to find. Additionally, they tend to be state-centric and have a variety of formats. While commonplace in the business world, archaeology has not developed what is called a data warehouse (Figure 3). However, one excellent program is the University of Arkansas' Center for Advanced Spatial Technologies (CAST) or what is called OpenGIS (see Carroll 2002). Overall, it is an axiom:

A collection of integrated, subject-oriented data which was collected in order to support decisionmaking in a particular activity or enterprise. Each unit in the warehouse is tested, relevant, and replicative. Data conform to established standards and operating principles.

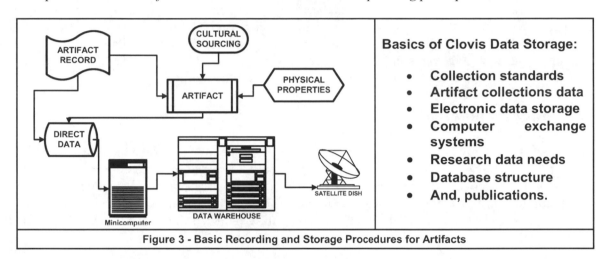

Figure 3 - Basic Recording and Storage Procedures for Artifacts

The McCary Survey fits this axiom nicely; it can be used for all archaeological investigations and prehistoric interpretations. What are needed here and archaeology in general, are data warehouse accesses. By this nature, archaeological research should be forced to find new ways of examining data, as Kantardzic (2003) suggests:

Thus, there is currently a paradigm shift from classical modeling and analyses based on first principles to developing models and the corresponding analyses directly from data.

This axiom is a process of collecting data from scientific observations and analyzing them, such as comparing these data to Clovis benchmarks (traits and metrics). The analysis from this process has always involved typical measures of central tendency, including mean, medium, mode, variance, and deviation. These factors tend to fall short of modern functional/structural analyses – they are simply *ole-tyme ways* of manipulating data. What remain from them are new ways to interpret data – such as forecasting methods, artificial intelligence (AI) methods, predictive modeling, data mining, and numerous techniques.

Collecting survey data is (and will be) one of the *fun* processes in archaeology. It allows hands-on examination and always presents something new – the basic romance of archaeology. While Clovis points[5] are more-or-less the same; they each tell a different story from the past. From its various recording operations, the McCary Survey has built a database from which more information about Paleoindian technology can be deduced than in any other state. The following analytical techniques (among many) are possible:

1 – Classification: creates groups of data in predetermined classes.
2 – Regression: maps data into real-time predictive variables.
3 – Clustering: identifies finite sets of data for descriptive methods
4 – Summarizing: provides generalities for datasets.
5 – Change: measures movement (differences) in variables, attributes, or types.

---

[5] Clovis is used here generically for all paleopoints.

6 – Deviation: measures change in variables, attributes, or types.
7 – Modeling: creates local (or broad-range) circumstances for data analysis.
8 – Boundaries: provides restrictive ranges (distribution) for data accumulation and analysis.
9 – Prediction: provides strategies for identifying unknown data or sites.
10 – Networking: uses artificial intelligence to recognize patterns (behavior) in data.

Certainly, other techniques are available and certainly new techniques will be invented. In one form or another, many of the techniques are used in Hranicky and McCary (1995) and Hranicky and Johnson (2005) which provide suggestions for future research. By placing Paleoindian data in a national data warehouse, this universe will be available for world-wide research. While Clovis is uniquely American, its appeal and fascination reach beyond our borders.

Defining a Model

A model is a tentative description of a system or events with a theory of the organization based on their properties. It is a hypothetical picture of the past that is based on a theoretical orientation and field-laboratory collected data. A model can be a numeric, graphic, or semantic presentation. Furthermore for archaeology, a model represents a proposed (hypothetical) picture of live (valid) data that was scientifically collected. In order to define a model, a requirements analysis should be performed.

The goals of this requirements analysis are to:

- Determine the data requirements of the database[6] in terms of artifacts
- Classify and describe the information about these artifacts
- Identify and classify the relationships among the artifacts
- Determine the types of transactions (research) that will be executed on the database
- Determine the interactions between artifact data and the transactions (research)
- Identify rules governing the integrity of the artifact data.

In archaeology, modeling has become a useful tool for site predictions, settlement patterns, and general cultural presentations. It has not become a regular tool in lithic technology because of the nature of lithic investigations which usually have a high level of diversity and interpretations. This is especially true for the use of graphical computer displays. As always, models have many forms; some are successful and others are failures. And, Clarke (1968) suggests:

Models may be involved in two different kinds of situations. In one category it is suggested that a certain model fits the archaeological situation under investigation and the aim is therefore to test the model for adequate fit or to obtain predictive information from it. Whereas, in the second category, the analyst has an archaeological system with a large amount of observed data and wishes to build a model to simulate the archaeological black box "behaviour".

More from Clarke (1968), three general models or frameworks are potentially useful in developing archaeological theory:

1 – Model for archaeological procedure - illustrating the three main spheres of archaeology as a discipline and setting out their procedure.

---

[6] Database is used here as a generic term for data storage. However, it is presently used in industry as a relational DB2 Universal Database which generally uses IBM's Native XML.

2 – Model for archaeological entities - the polythetic model as opposed to the tacit monothetic model of archaeological entities.

3 – Model for archaeological processes - archaeological entities changing with time as special kinds of dynamic systems susceptible to analysis in terms of general systems theory.

A survey model conforms to a set of preestablished rules, such as the scientific method. Also, it is a proposition based on logic, observations, constructive statements, data analyses, and offers predictions about certain data-set conditions. A model is an interpretation of a system from which we can define axioms (or hypotheses) based on observation, analysis, and study of that system. If the axioms are correct, the interpretation of the system must be correct. Changes in axioms or if axioms are found to be false (contradicted) cause a new model to be postulated. This also applies to premises; set of premises which, when taken together, are true. The model can also be used as a construct for a hypothesis. Basic models in lithic technology are:

1 – Settlement patterns
2 – Material procurement and tool construction
3 – Behavioral activities, such as hunting, etc.
4 – Cognitive conditioning – human life cycle social living.

Data models usually follow these forms:

- Logical data models (LDMs). LDMs are used to explore either the conceptual design of a database or the detailed data architecture of the survey. LDMs depict the logical data entities, typically referred to simply as data entities, the data attributes describing those entities, and the relationships between the entities.

- Physical data models (PDMs). PDMs are used to design the internal schema of a database, depicting the data tables, the data columns of those tables, and the relationships among the tables.[7]

- Conceptual data models. These models are typically used to explore domain concepts within archaeology. Conceptual data models are often created as the precursor to LDMs or as alternatives to LDMs.

Scientific models usually have the following organizations:

1 – Iconic model - it is a scaled or coded isomorphic record of observations which are presented as maps, graphs, or histograms. It is basically a reconstruction of data collected from an archaeological investigation; generalizing observations. The model is an excellent approach to displaying state-wide overviews of survey data.

2 – Analog model - it is the formulation of historic, anthropological (archaeological) data collected from empirical observations. It usually involves a time line and use of computational devices. The model is an excellent approach to define point morphologies and constructing classification standards.

---

[7] As used on relational databases, see Database Organization section.

3 – Symbolic model - it is a mathematical (statistical) presentation of numeric data collected from specific inquiries; for example, sampling excavated data. Probably the most common, this model allows data computations and comparisons to other survey data.

4 – Canonical model - logical presentations based on mathematical consequences of sampling; it proposes to approximate reality by the solution of a problem. It provides data for functional analyses. This model is ideal for testing hypothesis about database constructs which represent actual cultural situations in prehistory. This model follows a systems approach to organizing archaeological data.

These models are ideal candidates for using Model Views which are presented later. Obviously, there are numerous ways to model paleopoint data. However, the key is database availability and "already" having data in an electronic form. When point graphics are added to the survey database, then simulation models are possible.

Modeling and Simulation

Modeling and simulation analyses have been with archaeology for a long time – just lacking the computer. They are found in settlement patterns, procurement models, experimental archaeology, etc. Use of the computer speeds up calculations and processing, such as factor analyses; this type of computer-assisted research is increasing and offers unlimited testing and explanations for stone tools and their usage.

There are as many schemas to analyzing archaeological data as there are archaeologists. As a general guide, representation of tool data is based on its natural and physical structure or order. It has:

1 – Internal physical data - represents the tool's shape and design as they apply to the Laws of Nature

2 – External social data - represents the cultural world's influence and/or control on the tool's shape and design as they apply to the performance of task (work)

3 – Conceptual archaeological data - description of data that is independent of any cultural format

4 – Specific technology data - classification data based on industry or pan-Indian (even universal) tool forms.

5 – Function-centered data - based on universal human work/task-oriented survival activities.

6 – Structural design data – physical properties of a tool.

Once these data are placed in a context or organized archaeologically via site contexts and/or laboratory analyses, we have information about a culture at a particular time and place in prehistory. Data must be organized to obtain information. Naturally, it is the archaeologist who determines what data are collected and how these data are organized. But few archaeologists set up data structure definitions before organizing data. This definition determines the structure (intended use of the data) of the information.

Tool simulation is a multitechnical, multidisciplinal approach to replicating tool manufacture, performance, and usage in prehistory. There are no established methodologies and with new, everyday advances in computer technology, tool simulation will become a major focus in 21st century archaeology. It provides opportunities to create scenarios about actual tool operations in prehistory; comparative research data will open new doors to prehistoric interpretations and displays; the real past will be viewable by students and by the interested lay public.

Simulation techniques can be divided into two large categories, which are:

1 – Static: human factors are the controlling algorithms

2 – Dynamic: physical (Nature) factors are the controlling algorithms.

Scope of Knowledge

Knowledge is a fact-oriented acquisition that is extracted from sources of expertise, experimentation, empirical observations, scientific publications, and historic records. Knowledge can be called a knowledge base when it contains data in a specialized form. Or, a knowledge base is a collection of topic-related facts and one that is controlled by regulations (scientific method), such as concepts and terminology which have been accepted within a specific discipline or scientific specialty. For archaeology, the knowledge base usually has multidisciplinary sources.

Facts are usually collected by empirical observations; however, this computer age is producing electronically-collected data that often the researcher never sees personally. Once collected, these data are stored in a database where they can be processed to facts which become knowledge (Figure 4). Different processing produces different knowledge.

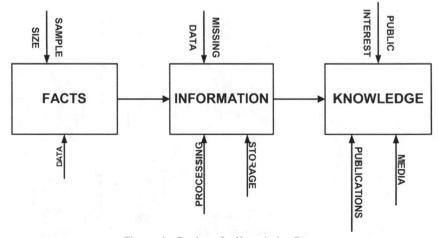

Figure 4 – Basics of a Knowledge Base

Archaeologically, the scope of knowledge has three forms:

- Published literature (basic form and source)

- Invisible college (knowledge shared within the archaeological and relic-world communities)

- Museum collection's information (static but available).

Knowledge can be classified in numerous ways, but a survey's knowledge is generally classified as:

1 – Declarative knowledge – is a descriptive representation of data and other relevant information. It presents facts of what "things" are. And, it assumes a relationship among all its collected data.

2 – Procedural knowledge – is a sequence-oriented presentation of acts or events. It is best known as "what ifs" and "cause-effect" knowledge.

3 – Process knowledge – is knowledge about knowledge, or the knowledge-based system within archaeology. It offers logic (or reasoning) capabilities which are often used as operational philosophies, such as technology evolution or diffusionist theories.

For archaeology, a knowledge base consists of documented knowledge based on field surveys and site excavations. Obviously, knowledge comes from other sources, but theoretically, it still must be integrated into the field-site knowledge base. Overall, this knowledge base could be called a knowledge domain, which in some ways, is restricted to the professional archaeological community.

While site-excavated points are included in surveys, the survey can claim membership (and contribution) in the knowledge base by arguing it is composed mainly of field collected data. Acceptance of its data is only as "good" as its Verification and Validation (V&V) procedures. This is why peer review works in mainstream archaeology; it should apply to the survey as well.

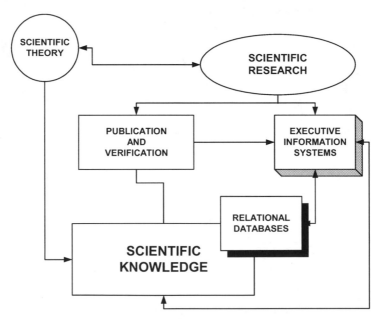

Figure 5 – Scientific Knowledge

Scientific Method – as for a survey, it is procedures that present exact objectives, factual, systematic, and acceptable methodologies in the study of prehistory. Overall, the method involves:

1 – Scientific theory and axioms
2 – Scientific research methods

16

3 – Work within the scientific community
4 – Verification of results
5 – Publication (history) of results
6 – Adding public knowledge to science.

By using the scientific method, the survey's objective to collect data and produce knowledge about the history of humanity has credibility in the archaeological community. Its principles are a scientific investigation of paleopoints for dissemination of data/information, which are based on ethical standards and practices, established procedures of observations, and validation of recorded resources (Figure 5).

Scientific Theory – as for the survey, it is the procedure that seeks an empirical, verifiable, and replicable explanation of cultural phenomena in an environmental setting. Survey data then becomes an explanation that is based on independent and disorganized data gathered from observations, experiments, and testing of processes which form, create, or otherwise influence the phenomena that archaeologists are investigating. Survey data are systematically integrated into a framework, which the investigator calls a theory. A theory can be based on function, structure, design, invention, or any number of meaningful patterns. For lithic technology, theory is an explanation of technological factors which affect toolmaking and tool usage.

Archaeological Knowledge Continuum

There are numerous forms of knowledge: scientific, theological, social, meta-physics, universal, personal, technical, etc. For archaeology, knowledge is essentially a continuum - the continuous acquisition of knowledge for the practicing members of the archaeological community. Each archaeologist contributes to the continuum by site investigations, artifact analyses, ethnographic studies, cross-cultural comparisons, theoretical interpretations, etc. The discipline builds on the work of former archaeologists to current archaeologists to future archaeologists who will study the knowledge we have gained so far. What is acceptable theory today may be replaced tomorrow.

All tools (entities) represent a knowledge base (or Indian real-world) in prehistory. In examining lithic tool production, the following can be asked:

1 – Are any attributes of tools so basic that they occur in almost every toolkit?

2 – Are there important relationships that exist among attributes in tool production?

3 – Is there a good set of primitive activities into which all knowledge can be broken down, such as tool kit basics (universals)?

4 – How should a toolkit be represented in that cultural world as opposed to another?

Quality Controls

Quality data means usability within the archaeological community. Few archaeological agencies, institutions, firms, and other organizations have quality control standards in place for governing their operations. Hranicky and Johnson (2005) were among the first to call for the use of quality standards based on ISO 9000 (International Standards Organization) which provides concepts and standards for quality management within an organization that delivers a product to the public trust or for public consumption. A survey complies with its verification, validations, and review processes. Collected data from appropriate sources must be analyzed to assess the suitability and effectiveness of its recording procedures and processes (see Link 2000). See Proof of Circumstances and Database Evaluation paragraphs below.

Archaeological Executive Systems

Discussing an Archaeological Executive Systems (AES) for archaeology is many squares away from an archaeological reality. While Executive Systems (ESs) are commonplace in the business and government worlds, the idea of providing archaeological resources and databases online is, perhaps, a lofty goal, but certainly one that will eventually come around to archaeology. Known by various names, for example, ES, Executive Support Systems (ESS), Decision Support Systems (DSS), Management Information Systems (MIS), and Executive Information Systems (EIS), these systems have one commonality – the integrations of large databases.

An AES would provide all three principal archaeological activities, namely academic, state/federal agencies, and contractual practices, with instant access to archaeological data, sites, reports, collections, and other contents in the archaeological world. From a Virginia perspective, site location access is possible,[8] but getting to contract reports requires a trip to the Virginia Department of Historic Resources in Richmond, Virginia. While there are published abstracts, published Virginia reports and papers occur all over the U.S. Getting copies is often more time consuming than the original research.

From a survey perspective, it would be only one small part of the AES, but when coupled with other artifact databases, a researcher could compare data/artifacts to known collections. The problem for creating an AES is reporting, terminology, classification schema, need to know, privacy acts, Native American rights, professional qualifications, virus protection, false data, and the list goes on… .

---

[8] Passworded, but available from Virginia's Department of Historic Resources.

Clovis Points as Entities

Most archaeologists would not refer to a Clovis point as an historical entity.[9] But, for a survey, the term entity has certain concepts that are ideal for setting up a survey, especially its database. An *Entity* is the principal data object about which information is to be collected. Entities are usually recognizable concepts, either concrete or abstract, such as the Clovis point or Paleoindian period. It is defined as in Hranicky (2004):

> **Entity** - object (artifact) of significance about which information (data, attributes, concepts, etc.) can be obtained which identifies the object so that it can be a standalone concept for all objects that meet its basic significance.

Most artifacts are not standalone entities in prehistory. Each, if viewed separately, tells only small parts of prehistory. However, rather than refer to an artifact as an item or object in normal archaeological concepts, the reference to it as an entity offers something of a totality in prehistory. An entity is any important or key object that represents history within itself – a standalone prehistorical object. Clarke (1968) suggests:

> *Entity is an integrated ensemble of attributes forming a complex but coherent and unitary whole at a specific level of complexity.*

Naturally, the first prerequisite of an entity is that it is a site-specific object; thus, it is dateable. Or, it is represented by numerous site-specific objects that are commonly known. Secondly, it represents completeness about its history. And thirdly, all entities are unique even though they represent the same history.

An entity involves numerous archaeological concepts, among which are:

1 – Types
2 – Classes (membership in an industry)
3 – Distinguishing forms among types
4 – Overlapping types
5 – Reference and intersection entities (association in archaeological contexts)
6 – Definition (description based on attributes)
7 – Volume or frequency over time (chronological frequencies)
8 – Distribution geographically (horizontal frequencies)
9   Event driven in its production
10 – Deteriorates out of existence over time (usage or loss of tradition)
11 – Result of creation processes (initializing as specific technology)
12 – Unique among other entities (attribute or trait set).

While the entity concept is quite similar to a type, it has a basic set of conventions that make it an ideal concept for lithic technology modeling. Type always implies evolution and/or change and includes numeric dimensions. An entity is a momentary definition of a lithic object. Theoretically, the conventions of one entity are not generally transferable to another entity, although the possibility exists, such as biface to biface. Each entity is unique but usually contains attributes from other class or type members. Its physical traits make it unique. We can assume redundancy, but a

---

[9] For most cases, the word artifact can be substituted for entity.

true entity has exclusivity based on some type of unique identifier(s), such as material, type of fabricator and, most importantly, the domain in which it is found (geography, time, culture, etc.).

An entity (object) always assumes completeness even though fragmentary, such as broken point or discard biface. Attributes for the entity can be optional or mandatory, but at least one must be unique so as to identify the object, such as fluting. Attributes can be ranked as primary, secondary, etc. and have measurable values/variables. Traits are entity specific and may or may not occur on other members of a class or type. These physical values or properties are never set by the maker (or researcher) but are derived at the instant the object came into being.

A derived attribute defines class and can be used to demonstrate ancestry, but as a caution, treat the entity as being unique; class as being a collection of entities sharing some type of attribute set. Regardless of its flaking pattern, the topography of each paleopoint is unique.

An entity must have:

1 – Attributes (two or more) - defines its type or class
2 – Trait set (more than n) - shows structure
3 – Relationships (at least one) - shows its heredity or ancestry
4 – Unique identifier (at least one) - establishes its history
5 – Function (at least one) - places it in a social usage context.

Any entity (object) always has traits. Depending on type/class definition, attributes describe the entity, but traits make it distinct from another entity. Relationship is, for the most part, a position outside the entity, such as time period or culture. The unique identifier is the attribute, such as shape, notch, flute, material, flaking, that makes it different from another type. Function is the purpose and/or usage of the entity. The assumption here is the manufacture of an entity was for a single function; subsequent usage may involve more than one function. Figure 6 shows the basic entity relationships.

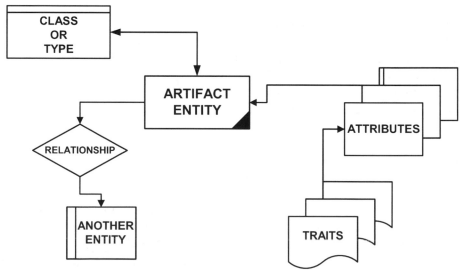

Figure 6 – Entity Relationships

Size or volume may be part of an entity, but this condition is not assumed to be a primary factor in establishing an entity. As a secondary factor, size could be a unique identifier. Entity is organized by topics in Table 2:

Table 2 – Entity Organizational Topics	
Association	Collecting data/information from several related entities
Category	Grouping entities by topic, class, domain, site, etc.
History	Using a hierarchy, such as time
Structure	Physical designs and morphology
Function	Work or task activities
Cardinality	Direction or cause/effect
Lifeways	A direct consequence in lifeways; a quality of life issue

Principles of an Entity

Based on an assumption that every entity is unique, the following apply:

☑ All entities are unique

☑ All entities are a single occurrence in prehistory

☑ An entity has an infinite number of traits

☑ All entities have technological legacies

☑ All entities have physical properties

☑ Every entity has one (primary) attribute that makes it unique

☑ All entities have a specific history and a generic (parent) hierarchy

☑ An entity has attributes found in other entities (relationship may or may not exist among entities)

☑ All attributes play a role of the entity of which they may not all be definable

☑ All entity roles can be assigned to a function

☑ All entity attributes are controlled by structure

☑ No entity can have two structural interpretations

☑ All entity attributes can have variables which collectively constitute that entity's domain

☑ All entities have a social definition.

Point Topology

Basically, topologists are mathematicians who study qualitative questions about geometrical structures. From an archaeological perspective, it is the study of form based on physical properties. This approach in defining projectile point shapes offers a new concept in archaeology. Additionally, it can be used on survey databases in which physical and graphic data have been stored. For an overview of topology, see Hatch (2002).

For a point surface's "characteristics," an algorithm is developed for describing its surface image. The output is a three dimensional graphic display which can be manipulated by the user. This aspect of modeling is beyond the scope of this publication. However, it is noted for advanced modeling studies and would include some of the following:

- Entities, such as point shapes
- Entities, such as curves in morphology
- Entities, such as surfaces
- Entities, such as volumes.

Two More Type and Class Definition

No topics in archaeology have received more attention and practice than typology and class, and two more short definitions are presented (as in Hranicky 2004).

Type - group of tools which have similar attributes which form a recognizable style or shape of the tool type. It is an implement that meets a specific form from predefined criteria; clustering of attributes. It is a basic unit of comparison and analysis of artifacts. It is a subdivision of artifact industry. Each type is a collection of attributes that presumably makes an artifact type different from another type. The typological concept is best defined in Krieger (1944), who advocated in his paper *The Typological Concept*:

Any group which may be labeled a type must embrace material which can be shown to consist of individual variations in the execution of a definite constructional idea; likewise, the dividing lines between a series of types must be based upon demonstrable historical factors, not, as is often the case, upon the inclinations of the analyst or the niceties of descriptive orderliness.

Class - group of artifacts, like points, knives, drills, etc., which can be broken down into recognizable categories, which are usually based on tool functions. Categories are a prerequisite of class. It is the template (mental image) or pattern (blueprint) for an object within a type. It is useful analytically because of its abstract properties, such as structured dimensions. Class should be a well-defined interface to the prehistoric world and is assumed to exist in a type.

Class in archaeology has a dual function. It defines a means for describing artifacts (entities) belonging to a class, and it defines the structure of a class. As a note: class is not transferable to another culture or time period without corrections or redefinitions. Class is culture specific. The problem lies with defining culture, namely all humanity has culture and culture occurs throughout history.

Major grouping of artifacts by any of these categories: structure, function, chronology, geography, special conditions, social purpose, design, and/or material; all of which can be subdivided into industries which is a grouping by function. Industries can be subdivided into types. All tools have a basic Final Manufacture Stage (FMS) function in production; thus, they have a single class assignment in archaeology.

For the survey, Paleoindian types have been established, but with some reservations on both their definitions and actual usage. Even Clovis as a type has wide-spread opinions as to what constitutes its definition as a type.

Additionally, this publication suggests that all types have benchmarks (attributes) which must be present on a point for its membership in a type. The type definition (attributes) offers a "what-if" for the physical properties (traits) of the point that is being studied. These what-ifs must be positive statements for the point under study, such as "is of," "is at," "is when," and numerous "what-if (is)" statements (Figure 7).

We can assume that a type is a member of a class/industry. Next, we assume that the type has certain attributes (benchmarks) which constitute the type.[10] Next, we assume that we can observe traits (landmarks) on the point in hand, and that the traits come close to the required attributes; thus, the point is typed. Same attributes can occur on numerous types, but benchmarks only occur on a specific type. Additionally, same traits can occur on numerous points, but landmarks only occur on a specific type.

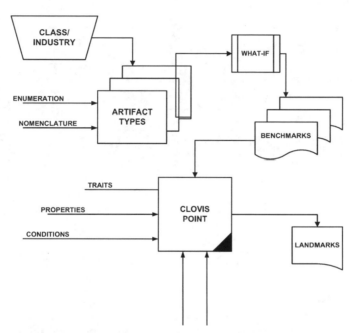

Figure 7 – Clovis Relationships to Typology and Class/Industry

---

[10] All types have attributes, but a specific type has benchmarks. Benchmarks are required, but attributes per se are not.

23

Database Organization

A survey is its database, which is a collection of interrelated data that is organized to meet the needs of archaeology and contribute to the Paleoindian knowledge base. It can be used by one or more persons and applied to numerous research categories and designs. Data organization always assumes that there are relationships among data and that by combining these data, information can be produced.

The principal output is the PC window which displayed selected fields or records (Figure 8). In addition to the primary output, the database's organization provides a systematic way to create knowledge via its data.

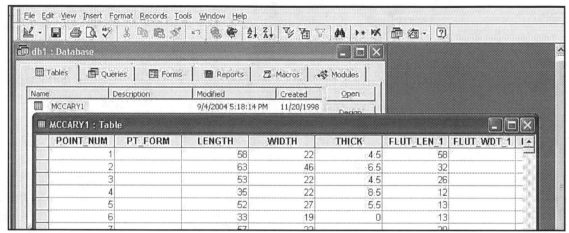

Figure 8 – Basic Survey Data Display

What "is/are" Data?

Data - as applied to scientific archaeology, is a collection of numerical or character symbols representing quantities, actions, observations, items, etc. from cultural resource investigations. Data are raw material for statistical analyses, all of which produce information. Data categories include but are not limited to:

1 – Date(s)
2 – Name(s)
3 – Relationship(s)
4 – Ownership
5 – Publication(s)
6 – Reference(s)
7 – Validity or Evaluations
8 – Provenance
9 – Lithic material(s)
10 – Functional description(s)
11 – Structural description(s)
12 – Cultural affiliation(s)
13 – Measurements
14 – Attributes
15 – Description(s).

For archaeology, most data fall into:

1 – Excavated data, or
2 – Nonexcavated data categories.

All excavated data is assumed to be prima facia evidence for scientific interpretations and publications. While this assumption is generally true, field collection biases, contaminations, and poor methodologies weaken this assumption. Data that are collected outside the excavated context always have lower validities, namely looted artifactual data and recovered data from destroyed sites. These data are called inference data. When data are related, they can be called a data set. The researcher must state sources and evaluate their impact on the interpretation.

A data set is defined as:

> **Data Set** - formal organization or grouping of raw data about lithic debris, tools, or artifacts. It is also a collection of all data from a particular project or investigation. Once data are arranged into a specific organization, the arrangement can be regarded as information. A data set can be an argument for an archaeological proof. A bound data set are data within a specific boundary (time and/or space). Contemporary data sets are digital in form and contain basic data and images.

For artifacts, it is:

☑ Presumption that a data set exists; namely, the group in which the item (object, tool, etc.) belongs is known.

It is a nonexploratory analysis, and the data set is usually displayed graphically or in tabular format.

Data are Facts?

One of the major criticisms of databases is that their contents (data) are too far from their represented object or entity. But in most cases, data are represented in research as facts from which knowledge is created.

Data are static representations for a class, type, attribute, trait, etc. which has an inheritance from some type of structure. Understanding them requires a meta-language based on some type of schema. By using a meta-language to read data, they can be mapped to a model or any research design. It is an iterative process, through a repeated cycle of analysis, design, and implementation – then start all over with the data set.

Data can be mapped …

When does data become facts? Data are only facts when the construct model is proven true. If for no other reason, this is the separation between traits and attributes. Attributes are simply not data; whereas, traits are always data. Attributes are based on proven data and are treated as fact, such as a flute, notch, etc. Attributes have no variable – a flute is a flute. Traits are always variables, such as flute length.

Which is a fact – flute or length? Flute is the fact, length does not exist. As such, are all facts physical objects? – yes. In this respect, facts constitute proofs or the physical evidences in archaeology.

Survey Organization for Data

For most survey organizers, the question arises – should the database be a standalone database or should it be configured with other institutional or agency databases? As long as the survey database is shareable, then it should be a standalone database which operates on a dedicated computer (or server). And, never data encrypt survey data – violates a public policy for the survey's database.[11]

A survey's data files are stored in a Database Management System (DBMS), such as created by Excel, Access, SQL, or Oracle. By complying with industry standards, a DBMS database can be moved to any new platform. Basically, a DBMS has:

- Update capabilities (adds, deletes, edits)
- Extract data from external sources (importing data)
- Queries and produces reports (interpretative outputs)
- Data security (controlling data sources and inputs)
- Data tracking (through a data dictionary, evaluation, and audit).

The DBMS is a standard operating system in archaeology and its mechanics are not discussed (see Larson 1995 and Turban and Aronson 2001 for overviews).[12] With today's computer systems, storage space is not generally a concern. However, numerous (dated/version) database backups must be maintained. Always run virus-checking software on the database's PC and server.

A DBMS is typically coupled with modeling software for statistical, mathematical, morphological object comparisons, extracting historical data, maintaining point locations, providing drill-down questions and answers, and numerous task-related computer operations. There are three typical DBMS structures: relational, hierarchical, and network. McFadden, et al. (1999) offers an overview of DBMS design and operation that is ideal for recordkeeping by surveys.

1 – Relational database – basically, it is a multiple spreadsheet design within the same database.

2 – Hierarchical database – orders data in a top-down fashion, such as the survey point numbering #1, #2, #3, etc.

3 – Network database – permits links among databases, including Internet sourcing (see Lattanzi (1999).

Four more advanced database designs are: object-oriented, multimedia, document-based, and intelligent databases; these often require a database manager. Use of these types of databases remains to be utilized in archaeology. Some federal and state agencies have these databases online for departmental access, but rarely for general public access. See Jameson (1997) and Appendix D provides a sample database design for a survey.

---

[11] In most states, regulatory legislation and industry standards mandate that confidential personal data be protected from unauthorized viewing, including from insiders without a legitimate "need to know." These regulations never apply to public database; thus, encryption is never needed.

[12] Survey data is usually time-stamped   date acquired. DB Rule: A data item reflects the status of an entity for a specified, bounded amount of time. When this time has expired, data items are considered to not be valid anymore. Survey data violates this rule. Old data are sometimes a basis for professional archaeology criticism. New Rule: Data are data – in the survey.

Database Evaluation

Every DBMS must be periodically tested and evaluated. This evaluation involves, but is not limited to:

- Record structures
- Field names, types, and sizes
- Relationships between records of different types
- Process making indexing for searches fast and efficient
- Equipment operating speeds and storage capacity
- And, other DBMS operations.

Evaluation records should be maintained to ensure successful maintenance and system upgrades. Evaluation testing and system monitoring is usually automated and performed at specified time/size/count intervals. Quality assurance (QA) practices also must be established for a survey.

Database Audit

While similar to database evaluation, an audit is used to find and correct database problems. It provides a validity trail (database history) which assists in maintaining V&V, ethical operations, and compliance with the survey's written policies, procedures, etc.

Auditing is the monitoring and recording of selected user database actions. Auditing is normally used to:

- Investigate suspicious activity. For example, if an unauthorized user is deleting data from tables, creating inappropriate files (such as dollar value), or adding unethical data, the survey administrator might decide to audit all connections to the database and all successful and unsuccessful deletions of rows from all tables in the database.

- Monitor and gather data about specific database activities. For example, the survey administrator can gather statistics about which tables are being updated, how many logical I/Os are performed, or how many concurrent users connect at peak times.

- Check data fields, indexing, and table structures to ensure they maintain survey standards and they meet correct database operations.

This audit assumes a system database format will have Open Database Connectivity (ODBC) so that it can be accessed by other database systems. As a major audit problem, should the survey's database be a distributed system where database copies are placed on independent systems, such as on state agencies or academic institution computer systems.

Auditing is site autonomous; an instance of audits (time stamped) only with statements issued by directly connected users at a specific time. A local survey cannot audit actions that take place in a remote database. Because remote connections are established through the user account of a database link, the remote audit is not possible through the database link's connection. In other words, a remote database may not contain the same data as the base survey's database. The recommendation: a remote survey database should be **read-only** for its users.

Structured Query Language (SQL)

Structured Query Language (SQL) is the set of commands and operations that all programs and database administrators must use to access data in an Oracle database. Application programs and Oracle tools often allow users access to the database without using SQL directly, but these applications in turn must use SQL when executing the user's request. While other database managers can be used, SQL is recommended. For most large commercial databases, SQL is the primary manager.[13]

Oracle SQL complies with industry-accepted standards and easily meets all archaeological needs. Oracle Corporation ensures future compliance with evolving SQL standards by actively involving key personnel in SQL standards committees. Industry-accepted committees are the American National Standards Institute (ANSI) and the International Standards Organization (ISO), which is affiliated with the International Electrotechnical Commission (IEC). Both ANSI and the ISO/IEC have accepted SQL as the standard language for relational databases. When a new SQL standard is simultaneously published by these organizations, the names of the standards conform to conventions used by the organization, but the standards are technically identical. Connolly and Begg (2005) and Kifer, Bernstein, and Lewis (2005) provide discussions on SQL databases.

The latest SQL standard published by ANSI and ISO is often called SQL92 (and sometimes SQL2). The formal names of the new standard are:

- ANSI X3.135-1992, "Database Language SQL"
- ISO/IEC 9075:1992, "Database Language SQL."

SQL92 defines four levels of compliance: Entry, Transitional, Intermediate, and Full. A conforming SQL implementation must support at least Entry SQL. Oracle8, Release 8.0, fully supports Entry SQL and has many features that conform to Transitional, Intermediate, or Full SQL.

Oracle8 conformance to Entry-level SQL92 was tested by the National Institute for Standards and Technology (NIST) using the Federal Information Processing Standard (FIPS), FIPS PUB 127-2.

What is a Relational Database?

A relational database stores all its data inside tables, and nothing more. All operations on data are performed on the tables or the action produces another table. A table is a collection of data which is organized in a certain way.

A table is a set of rows and columns. This is very important because a data set does not have any predefined sort order for its elements. Each row is a set of columns with only one value for each. All rows from the same table have the same set of columns, although some columns may have NULL values, i.e., the values for that row was not initialized. Note that a NULL value for a string column is different from an empty string. A NULL value should be an "unknown" value.

The rows from a relational table are analogous to a record, and the columns to a field or a specific data entry item. The following is an example of a table and the SQL statement that creates the table:

---

[13] SQL does permit open user access via Microsoft's Open Database Connectivity (ODBC).

```
CREATE TABLE MCCARY_SURVEY (
        ARTIFACT char(30),
        COUNTY char(20),
        TYPE char (25)
)
```

```
+--------------------+---------------+------------------------+
| ARTIFACT           | COUNTY        | TYPE                   |
+====================+===============+========================+
| Fluted Point       | Scott         | Clovis                 |
+--------------------+---------------+------------------------+
| Notched Point      | Fairfax       | Palmer                 |
+--------------------+---------------+------------------------+
```

Survey Database Design

The essential aspect of designing a survey database is the logical structure of its data. Design defines how data are classified and related and, most importantly, a set of rules for data structure, access rights, updating, deletion, and numerous other database functions. Design involves six phases:

- Analysis
- Creation
- Development
- Implementation
- Maintenance
- Output.

Analysis

Analysis requires creating a conceptual data model that describes survey and its data. This model provides requirements for the design and its specifications. Next, a process flow is created.

Creation

Creation provides the logic for the database and conforms to DBMS normalization. Next, an input and out put process is created. Data in both these conditions are temporary in contrast to what is actually stored in the database.

Development

Development is the creation of the database. It requires conventional programming, testing, and evaluation. If an off-the-shelf product is purchased, it is simply a process of learning how to operate the software.

Implementation

Implementation places the three previous phases into use by the survey. It involves loading "live" data and testing the database's operation.

<u>Maintenance</u>

Maintenance is a database requirement to ensure that the system operates as expected – over time. It also includes backups and software upgrades.

<u>Output</u>

The survey's output is usually in an electronic format. As recommended, output should include Excel and Access formats because some users do not have access to high-level database managers, such as SQL or Oracle. Standard DBMS organization is required for cross-platforms continuity.

Normalizing Survey Data

A survey database must follow widely accepted standard called data normalization. Normalization is essentially a two step process that puts data into tabular form by removing repeating groups and then removes duplicated data from the relational tables. Most surveys can be designed initially to have relational tables, such as basic metrics, provenances, or ownership. Table 3 provides normal forms needed for a survey database.[14]

Table 3 – Database Normal Forms	
Form	**Description**
First Normal Form	A relational table, by definition, is in first normal form. All values of the columns are atomic. That is, they contain no repeating values.
Second Normal Form	The definition of second normal form states that only tables with composite primary keys.
Third Normal Form	The third normal form requires that all columns in a relational table are dependent only upon the primary key.

Database Versions

All survey databases should be labeled by a version schema, such as DB_11_2004. These versions should be backed up and stored. In an event of a system crash, the survey director can revert to a previous version which will minimize data loss.

Database Monitoring

Database monitoring provides service-based database monitoring (monitoring database response times from an end-user's perspective) and server-based database monitoring (monitoring database server integrity and availability). The end goal of database monitoring is to ensure the database is always available and running at peak performance so it does not compromise the archaeological services it supports. Database monitoring when tied to content monitoring, ping monitoring, port monitoring, access monitoring, and server monitoring provides a high level of assurance that the site is operational. They are:

- Content monitoring ensures your content has not been altered, and your content delivery mechanism is working properly.

---

[14] There are currently five normal forms that have been defined. For a survey, the first three normal forms that were defined by E. F. Codd (original IBM database designer) are used.

- Ping monitoring ensures the network device -- switch, hub, router, server, etc. -- is alive.

- Port monitoring ensures the application or service running on a given IP address and port is running.

- Access monitoring ensures that only authorized users have rights to the database. Even with a public policy, databases must be monitored for security.

- Server performance monitoring ensures you know about issues causing your server to perform poorly and slowly.

Monitoring is recorded in a systems' operational log, which maintains dates, names, and specific database operations. In the case of using SQL, a roll-back can be performed in case of a major database failure on the part of uses and equipment breakdowns. Server performance monitoring involves answering the following questions:

- Is the CPU being overrun?
- Am I running out of disk space?
- Do I have enough real memory (RAM) and swap space?
- Is my server load too high?
- Do I have the ability to plug in an unlimited number of scripts [15]using any scripting language?
- Does my monitoring protect all avenues of failure?

Now you can create your own monitoring events and have the ability to restart services and more. Restoration is the primary reason for database monitoring; failure to do so can mean a "lot" of data reentry time. Basic monitoring requires "best" administrative practices.

Small databases can avoid the need for monitoring if they are not always online, do not have outside access, or are backed up after each data entry session. For large databases or integrated systems, monitoring involves setting alarms and perhaps automatic shutdowns. The principal defense is the use of a firewall to protect the systems from unauthorized entry. Naturally, all database/systems should have automatic virus monitoring.

Data Warehouse

Without going into the "nuts and bolts," a data warehouse system is needed for American archaeology. Far too much data and reports are stored in state-centric libraries which are impossible to locate and access. Thus, in many cases, the archaeological wheel is re-inventing "time discoveries" again and again. At least, there are efforts to nationalize fluted point data (see Hranicky and Johnson 2005 for a discussion). For the federal government and large-corporate business world, this process is evolving into Enterprise Architectures (EAs). Again, this topic is too complex for this publication. However, the basics are:

- Subject-oriented data
- Integrated data
- Nonvolatile data (survey data)

---

[15] Scripts are machine instructions that perform special actions on a database; they vary from system to system and depend on user/server needs.

- Data remains fixed (nonstatic)
- Longer time between data refreshing
- Detailed and summary data
- Used solely for scientific purposes.

The major problem in data warehousing is coordinating databases, providing hardware, and database maintenance. A factor that is used here is real-time operation and updating legacy (old) systems and databases. Data warehousing involves client-server operations which, simply by the implications, leave archaeology far behind the other scientific disciplines.

A topic that has received little attention in archaeological databases is virtual reality modeling (VRM). With the use of Webpages, VRM allows displays of Clovis points in a form that is only available to the giants of networking. VRM is easily a decade away in archaeology. VRM can also be called object-oriented simulation. VRM should be a basic goal for surveys.

Related to VRM, simulation modeling allows the database to be used for conducting what-if and cause-effect experiments and their analyses. Like VRM, simulation is a descriptive process that has no optimal solution. Once values, metrics, data, events, processes are assembled, the best among several alternatives can be selected. The controlling factor in creating VRMs and simulations is complexity, such as too many variables, formulations are too large, or simply a model cannot be constructed with any degree of success.

In the past, factor analysis (as in: Blalock 1972), and currently, multivariate statistics (as in Tabachnick and Fidell 2001), and discriminate analysis (as in Klecka 1980) were a common method for analyzing artifact data, but their adherence to mathematical relationships did not adequately explain changes. Relationships among variables, traits, and attributes were restricted to a pre-determined hierarchy that, while mechanistic, did not identify a cause-effect relationship among point factors, namely material, fluting, and dimensional variables. Overall, the total survey point population is not presented as a change process. Thus, a researcher simply could not measure change processes, such as adaptation, material changes, or regional dispersions of style. The survey has, and will always have, chronology problems with its data. However, if analyses are modeled to look for cause-effect factors, a structural model of a state's points can be built up using existing data. The survey comes closer to baselining paleopoints than any other large-scale Paleoindian technology investigations.

Verification & Validation (V&V)

Probably the biggest concern with a survey within the professional archaeological community is the validity of its data? And as an answer, the survey by nature of its operation will always have validity problems. Presumably, the larger the database is, the less of a problem with data validity. V&V always assumes that credibility and quality assurance are priorities in recordation. It is an evaluation process that is based on some type of expert analysis that produces high reliability for V&V. Additionally, the V&V focus produces point authentication (collectors) from which data can be extracted.

The major consequence for V&V is the non-personally found artifact. Far too many "good" points are available at relic shows and on the Internet. For these "good" specimens, someone is always "testifying: to the point's credibility and authenticity when he/she has no first-hand knowledge of the point's discovery. This acquisition and subsequent recoding violates a First Principle for the survey's operation. See Principles for Survey Operation section.

Table 4 provides V&V concerns for recorded points. V&V is defined as:

Validation – evaluation of a survey that it conforms to acceptable standards in archaeology.

Verification – evaluation of a survey that it is correctly implemented using standards in archaeology.

Table 4 – Survey Concerns for Validation and Verification (V&V)	
Point Concern	Survey Solution
Accuracy	Ensuring that the database reflects reality
Adequacy	Ensuring that appropriate and complete data are collected
Availability	Ensuring that survey data are available to scholarly research
Completeness	Ensuring that all data fields are complete with accurate data. Queries often rely on completeness (see Demolombe 1996 and 1997)
Data collection	Using established procedures to collect data
Data management	Ensuring that the database is operated and maintained using established computer industry standards and procedures
Disjunctive sources	Avoiding any point sourcing (fabrications) that is not verifiable
Ethics	Ensuring that the survey maintains the highest level of professional ethics
Fake points	Using experts and scientific methods on authenticating points
First hand reporting	Verifying and assessing the credibility of the contributor
NIGRPA	Ensuring there is no violation
Measurement precision	Using established scientific techniques
Methods	Following accepted scientific methodologies
Monetary	Avoiding any assessment or recognition of dollar values
Openness	Recording any legitimate point from anyone
Point classification	Using established survey standards
Point validation	Using experts for authentication
Point verification	Using experts for certification
Precision	Ensuring all measurements are accurate
Provenance	Using the credibility of the source for determining originating location
Public data	Ensuring that all survey data is made public and part of the public realm
Publication	Ensuring that all accepted points are published
Quality	Ensuring that recoded data meets consistency and conforms to normalized data standards
Recording points	Using established procedures and methods
Reliability	Ensuring sources have credibility
Requirements	Ensuring that all data collection meets survey written policies, procedures, practices, and standards
Resources	Ensuring that the survey has resources to collect and preserve data
Second hand reporting	Using common sense for acceptance
Site looting	Promoting site preservation
Sourcing contacts	Ensuring that points come from credible individuals and that the point meets all legal requirements

Usefulness	Ensuring that collected data meets standards in archaeology
Updated data	Ensuring that survey data are updated when new information or techniques become available
Value added	A consequence of the survey; not promoting it as a recording factor

A set of operational principles can assist data V&V by guiding point recording procedures. Principles are discussed later. Also, lessons learned based on McCary Survey operations are presented in the Lessons Learned chapter.

Data V&V

While all positive efforts are made to record paleopoints accurately, errors do occur. One way to "catch" these errors is during the data entry process. The computer can be set (flags) to check all entries and ensure that they fall within the range of expected norms. Paleopoints have benchmarks and when data entry attempts to violate them, an error checking process notifies the recorder of the error. Depending on the circumstances, the error-flag can be overwritten; for other cases, data entry can be rejected entirely. Error checking is a major way to ensure V&V for a survey's database.

As part of V&V, data integrity has two major requirements to meet:

- Standards and proofs within the archaeological community
- Standard database operations within the computer industry.

Equipment V&V

Periodic equipment testing is needed for all the survey's electronic test equipment and recording devices. Maintenance (hardware/software) activities are defined into four categories:

- Administrative – support of the software product or resources to ensure compliance with equipment life cycle model

- Corrective – standard problems, bug fixes, or part failures

- Adaptive – modifications to the software/hardware stemmed from changes to the infrastructure or operating environment

- Perfective – modifications to allow the software/hardware to meet new survey requirements.

Proof of Circumstances

Frequently, data collection for a survey is based on "word-of-mouth sources. And, as a consequence, V&V is heavily dependent on the survey's proof that the recording source meets reasonable expectations from the archaeological and relic worlds. A survey should meet validity evidence requirements for scientific research.

The following are ways to check data entry:

- Survey data form review before data entry
- Computer input checking
- Database normalizing

- Model clarification of data requirements
- Data integrity[16] (see Appendix D – Database Design)
- Entity composition (specific trait/attribute requirements)
- Numerous other possibilities (see DB administrator's guide books).

These proofs are basic to quality control for the survey's general operations. There is no 100% guarantee for data quality, even for those collected from the professional archaeological community. For archaeological research using survey data, sufficient accumulated **validity** evidence is available for a selection procedure to justify its use in a new research without conducting a local validation research study. By following written procedures, etc., V&V provides data integrity for the survey and its use in archaeology.

Data Certainty

All archaeological investigations are the result of numerous variations in expertise, interpretation, and methodology. Even so, certainty of the data and artifactual interpretation contains a professional acceptance that approaches *an archaeological truth*. While the overall field of knowledge may be regarded as proofs, it fails as an expert field (such as physics and chemistry). At best, data certainty is:

☑ Since the order in which archaeological evidence is collected is arbitrary, data certainty is commutative and associative, which is based on the overall practice of the discipline.

☑ Until total archaeological certainty is reached, additional confirming archaeological evidence must be increased via new data.

☑ If contemporary archaeological evidences are chained together, the result is a tentative certainty based on inferences from data.

Once artifactual data have associated data produced by other scientific means (C14, etc.), certainty can be said as positive statements. If written standards, policies, and procedures are in place in an agency, institution, or organization, data certainty is greatly enhanced by validation accreditation of the above operating practices.[17]

We know the existence of an entity before we know anything about it...

---

[16] Data integrity is one of the cornerstones of the survey model. Simply stated, data integrity means that the data values in the database are correct and consistent.

[17] Negative statements in archaeology are always unknowns and never supported by data.

Principles for Survey Operation

As suggested, there are no hard-and-fast rules for the operation of a survey. State surveys are usually run cooperatively by amateur and professional archaeologists; thus, skill and talent vary. Regardless, the survey manager must have the practical expertise to identify and analyze paleopoints and have the competency to maintain the survey's database. Furthermore, survey operations must follow established principles that maintain survey integrity and basic archaeological ethics. The following suggestions are survey basics for creating principles:

- Person submitting the point must be the legal owner[18]
- Point must be publishable
- Only one survey per state
- Roll-up state data to a national database
- A survey review committee to review points
- Encourage state-museum Clovis collections
- Provide survey data to all scholars
- Encourage collector participation
- Use the WEB for public access
- Survey governance is a form of public trust.

The McCary Survey adheres to a fundamental set of operating principles intended to ensure that point recording is of the highest quality and makes a substantive contribution to enhancing the archaeological science, lithic technology, and promotes public appreciation and understanding of Paleoindian technology. The following operating principles influence every aspect of recording and analyzing Paleoindian points.

First Principle involves the basic accession of points from which all point data are recorded. There may be preliminary curation, but certainly, the total recordation process is performed. All data recording is from first-hand observations; a verification process. This principle is essential for survey data validity and completeness.

Second Principle moves to the next phase by taking all collected data and formulating it into information about the point. This principle involves classifying the point into a class, but preferably, a type. This is a structure or morphological method. All data are compiled using standard nomenclatures based on validation practices. It relies on a review process for collected data and interpretations.

Third Principle provides that the point be combined with other points in a type to foster the creation of a cultural setting. The focus generally involves incorporating the point into established, known cultures for specific geographies. This principle also involves establishing function for the point. As data are published using an established typology and using verification & validation (V&V) testing, database accuracy and integrity will be a standard for third principle archaeology.

These principles provide a survey with quality conformance to record, manage, and track paleopoint data. They improve performance which enhances the survey's operation and acceptance within the archaeological community.

---

[18] The acceptance of a point into the survey should only be allowed for the person who finds the point or the archaeologist who excavated the point. See Lessons Learned section.

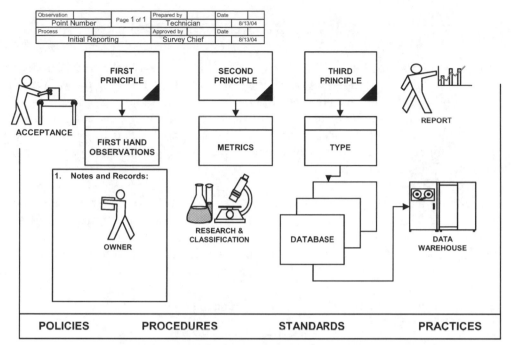

Figure 9 – Relationships of Principles and Overall Operations

These principles are operational concerns and do not represent a work or process flow. The basic philosophy of these principles is that they exist to describe the physical universe of Paleoindian technology. The key word is "describe." First principle is a paradigm of direct observations on phenomena; in this case, artifacts, their data, and contexts. Data are collected from these observations and analysis of them is what can be called *first-hand* study of the phenomena. Figure 9 shows an overview of recording paleopoints based on principles that reflect research methodologies – which are based on established standards, policies, practices, and procedures.

The second principle leads to the scientific methodology for point recording. It represents the metrics of the survey procedures. The third principle leads the recorded points to established point types.

Survey Implementation

Implementing can be defined simplistically as getting a newly developed set of survey procedures in place for those persons who want a state's paleodata. It starts with the original suggestion through a feasibility study (establishing needs), system analysis and design programming, training, conversion or collection methods, and finally implementation and operation. While the survey could simply be maintained on index cards, the super computer age brings data processing to almost a standalone intelligent system of hands-off operation. On the face of it, recording points should be a simple operation, then again…

For states without any type of paleopoint surveys, an implementation plan should be drafted and circulated in the professional/archaeological, collector, and museum communities. It serves as an intent to implement but, most importantly, will generate feedback that opens undiscovered doors before the implementation process begins. It is the world of Native American artifacts (Figure 10).

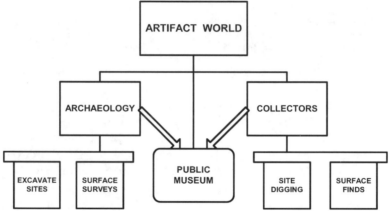

Figure 10 - Archaeology and the Relic World. At least something from the past comes to the present and is preserved for the future. Then, there is the Native American view of their material culture history and its preservation. And, it is amazing that Nature can preserve sites and artifacts for thousands of years and man/womankind can destroy them in a matter of seconds. Hopefully, at least part of the recovered prehistoric world makes it into public museums, institutions, and agencies.

The following are basic considerations for implementing a survey:

1 - Implementation Issues

A survey should establish communications within the archaeological community and define its activities, availability, and who will manage the survey. Conveying this information can avoid implementation issues, especially survey management and operation.

2 - Point Sources

The survey operates with/from submitted points from the archaeological and collecting communities. Implementing a survey requires notification and justifying the survey to an intended audience, hopefully those who will support it. Initially, a survey needs to recruit point submissions.

3 - Exacting Provenances

The science of archaeology is based on the in situ artifact. Time and space correlations provide data for historical interpretations. While every attempt is made in a survey to exact provenance from submitted paleopoint owners, few are ever recorded with GIS accuracy. The basic cause is the point "handlers" are usually nonprofessionals, and there is a failure to understand the significance of exact point provenance.

4 - Organization Factors

Survey implementation may threaten the archaeological organization of the professional and amateur societies. Thus, a survey should not be neutral, but should strive to become part of the archaeological community. The survey must remain compatible and maintain goals that accommodate archaeology.

5 - Management Practices

The survey needs a director and may need minor volunteer support. Other positions are the database manager and a publication specialist. For most surveys, these are not paid positions; thus, it needs hosting and funding. Implementation for these roles must be worked out before the actual survey operations begin.

6 - Technical Factors

Technical factors are computer hardware/software and measuring implements needs for the survey's operation. Technical issues are:

- Constraints, which result from the limitation of data processing technology
- Technical problems, which result from a scarcity of resources
- Technology resources for analyzing points.

7 - User Factors

Users are those who support the survey by participating in its operation and those who use its resources for research and public displays and education. Establishing users are an essential factor for a successful survey.

8 – Database Design and Issues

A survey is its database. Database design should be performed by someone who has experience in this specialty. How and by whom it is administered should be established before implementation. However, its location and hosting (if any) are part of the survey setup.

9 - Values and Ethics

The goals of a survey must contain ethics procedures and policies that follow archaeological practices and standards. Thus, implementation must ensure that the survey has a contribution to the archaeological knowledge base and its practices meet archaeology's ethical standards.

10 – Knowledge Base Factors

Once a survey is created and perhaps before implementation, the survey should be connected to whatever knowledge base(s) exists at that time. Additionally, connection(s) to networks, internet, or database services should be made.

11 – <u>Implementation Strategy</u>

Probably the best approach to implementation is to present the survey as an expert system that is governed by professionals who will produce high-quality information. This involves:

- Quality of the survey operation
- Cooperation in the archaeological community
- Acceptance or justification for survey operation.

There are numerous factors in creating and implementing a survey. Probably the major problem that arises is the politics of the archaeological community which the survey serves. Once past who will manage and administer the survey, most of the above categories will be easy to accomplish.

12 – <u>Defining Survey Users</u>

For most surveys, access is free and unrestricted. However, the survey should find scholars who perform Paleoindian research and keep them informed of survey inputs and outputs.

> **Following McGimsey's (1972) publication: *Public Archaeology*, all survey data are part of the public realm and are available to anyone who wishes to use them for scholarly studies.**

Survey Lessons Learned

The McCary Survey provides numerous lessons learned from its operational history. Some of them are presented in Table 7. It provides very generic topics and survey actions; actual events cannot be published here. Most of a survey's operation is commonsense, providing a data-only philosophy is followed. This publication reflects the organizational learning in the McCary Survey's operation; perhaps a written document for lessons learned should be maintained by a survey, which would contain names, dates, actions, and responses. This information may violate confidentiality, but it should be made public, only if asked!

Point Finder-Only Rule

Based on the McCary Survey, point reporting by collectors who did not find the point does, in most cases, cause a problem for V&V of the point. As a suggested rule, a survey should only record points where the owner can certify that he/she actually found the point – the Point Finder-Only Rule. If an owner can provide written proof of his/her obtaining the point from someone else who found it, then that point would be acceptable. Otherwise, points outside this property factor are suspect and should not be recorded.

Table 7 – Lessons Learned form the McCary Survey	
Lesson	**Learned Activity**
Get archaeological support	A survey needs (must have) support and participation from the professional archaeological museum communities.
Set goals for the survey	A survey must have goals and objectives to survive. It must have a purpose that supports the archaeological community.
Capturing point data	A survey must have standards for capturing point data
Expert analysis	A survey must have experts for analyzing and recording points
Produce publications	A survey is not a self-serving organization; therefore, it must publish frequently the points that have been recorded.
Provide benefits	A survey must provide benefits to archaeological research and provide data to the public knowledge about paleopoints
Provide education	A survey must approach the general public to educate them about archaeology and its need for information about prehistory
Provide preservation information	A survey must approach the general public to educate them about archaeology and its need for preservation of prehistoric antiquities
Acceptance policy	A survey must have a written policy regarding its criteria for accepting (or rejecting) a point into the survey
Avoid cost	In order for a survey to remain independent, it should not be funded by public dollars
Setting point values	A survey must avoid any type of monetary assessment of point values
Survey access	A survey must provide public access

Looting observation	A survey must report knowledge of site looting, but take no role in stopping it
Meeting ethical requirements	A survey must publish polices that meet or exceed those set by the Society for American Archaeology
Responding to Native Americans	A survey should keep Native Americans in its coverage area informed of the survey's activities and goals
Maintaining public polices	A survey's rule: no private archaeology and all data are part of the public realm
Fake point submissions	A survey will always be faced with this problem
Nonstate submissions	A survey will always be faced with this problem
Point classification	Survey personnel should never force a point into a Paleoindian type; it either has the attributes, or it does not
Review responses	All survey review committee reports must be in writing.
Changing hands	Survey points will change hands and, in many cases, the survey will never see them again.
Hand-written records	McCary's hand-written notes for the Survey may have survived, but are not currently available. Copies of these materials should be backed up as they represent a history of the Survey's operation.
Point loss	Quite simply, points get broken and lost and are not always available for restudy by the survey or archaeologists.
Recording variation	Every recorder sees a paleopoint differently; there is always a difference in opinions about a paleopoint.
Quality controls	All practices and processing of points and data must conform to established quality control standards to ensure consistency and uniformity in survey data.

Curation Processes

As presented and repeating, a survey is a knowledge-based operation; it is not an artifact acquisition operation. From a survey viewpoint, artifacts exist solely for their data which are turned into point information. However, a survey cannot be totally outside artifact curation. Private collections do change ownerships which may be to the detriment of a state's archaeological responsibility. As suggested, a survey must not own artifacts; on occasion, it can recommend ownership, provided there are no monetary costs involved in the transactions.

Probably the most notable reason why a survey would be involved in point ownership is its casual discovery – surface finds. Some owners simply want their points to go into the public realm so that scholars may study them. In this case, the survey would recommend institutions, public agencies, or academic institutions for their home. The survey only becomes involved if the artifact's transfer is on a gift basis. Appendix F provides a Deed of Gift example.

All curation processes and methods should be based on the American Association of Museums (AAM) guidelines and recommendations. Most Americans view museums as the most trusted institution in our society. Obviously, a good working relationship with all state museums benefits the survey's reputation and participation in the study of antiquities.

Clovis Point Repository[19]

Fluted point discoveries throughout the East are numerous. Most of the discoveries are lifetime finds which leave owners somewhat in estatia (estate from the past) with its ownership, but at the same time, worried about being a temporary custodian of an item that is 10,000 years old. While local museum and state archaeological agencies provide homes for prehistoric artifacts, specialized collections are generally not maintained or displayed. The answer is a fluted point repository where people can donate single (or multiple) finds. Their name remains with the point, and he/she gains a high degree of confidence that their donation is now in the public realm – a contribution to maintaining part of our history for the future. A repository would be open to anyone and accept fluted points from all over the U.S. As an example, its charter would state in part (Hranicky 2003):

> A Repository will be a secure location for citizens to place their fluted points found in (specific state) and will allow the placement of points from other states. These points are considered national cultural treasures which will be saved for the future. All points will be recorded in the state Survey; furthermore, no point will be added to the Repository unless it has been accepted and recorded in the state Survey. Out-of-state points must have a Certificate of Authenticity, commonly called COAs. The Survey staff (committee) will be available to assist in evaluations of its contributions. A Repository is restricted to Paleoindian lanceolate points/bifaces as defined by various state professional organizations. All points will be maintained and displayed (where possible) in the name of the donor, if so requested. The repository should be located at a secure facility. Due to the high value nature of fluted points, an annual audit will be conducted.

For an overview of artifact repositories, see Sullivan and Childs (2003), King (1980), or Terrell (1979).

---

[19] A candidate would be the state archaeological society.

Survey Ethics

By the very nature of any survey operation, a problem exists with perceived ethical conduct within the archaeological community. A survey should have a written policy which deals with ethics, and how the survey complies with them. A major ethical problem within archaeology is the commercial privatization of data by contracting/consulting firms. The answer is not here, but see Appendix H. The following references can be used as a guide.

U.S. Department of the Interior
(2002) Looting – A Global Crisis. Cultural Resource Management, Vol. 25, No. 2, Washington, DC.

Society for American Archaeology
(1994) Save the Past for the Future II: Report of the Working Conference. Washington, DC.

Lynott, Mark J. and Alison Wylie
(1995) Ethics in American Archaeology: Challenges for the 1990s. Society for American Archaeology, Washington, DC.

Broodie, Neil, Jennifer Doole and Colin Renfrew (eds.)
(2001) Trade in Illicit Antiquities: the Destruction of the World's Archaeological Heritage. McDonald Institute Monographs, University of Cambridge, Cambridge, Eng.

Vitelli, Karen D. (ed.)
(1996) Archaeological Ethics. AltaMira Press, Walnut Creek, CA.

Wormington, Hannah Marie
(1966) The Spirit of Worthwhile Collecting. Chesopiean, Vol. 4, Nos. 4-5, pp. 134-36.

Krech, Shepard III, and Barbara A, Hill (eds)
(1999) Collecting America, 1870 – 1960. Smithsonian Institution Press, Washington, DC.

Renfrew, Colin
(2000) Loot, Legitimacy and Ownership. Duckworth Debates in Archaeology. Bookcraft (Bath) Ltd, Midsomer Norton, Avon, GB.

Board of Directors
(2000) Code of Ethics & Practice of Interest to Museums. American Association of Museums, Washington, DC.

New York State Association of Museums
(1974) The Ethics and Responsibilities of Museums with Respect to Acquisition and Disposition of Collection Materials. New York State Association of Museums, Troy, NY.

International Council of Museums (ICOM)
(1987) Code of Professional Ethics, In ICOM Statues/Code of Professional Ethics, ICOM, Maison de l'Unesco, Paris, France.

Department of the Interior
(1993) Museum Property Handbook, Volume I, Preservation and Protection of Museum Property. U.S. Department of the Interior, Washington, DC.
(1997) Policies and Standards for Managing Museum Collections. Departmental Manual, Part 411, U.S. Department of the Interior, Washington, DC.

King, Thomas
(1998) Cultural Resource Law and Practice. AltaMira Press, Walnut Creek, CA.

Society for American Archaeology Ethical Statement

At its April 10, 1996 meeting, the SAA Executive Board adopted the Principles of Archaeological Ethics, reproduced below, as proposed by the SAA Ethics in Archaeology Committee. The adoption of these principles represents the culmination of an effort begun in 1991 with the formation of the ad-hoc Ethics in Archaeology Committee. The committee was charged with considering the need for revising the society's existing statements on ethics. A 1993 workshop on ethics, held in Reno, resulted in draft principles that were presented at a public forum at the 1994 annual meeting in Anaheim. SAA published the draft principles with position papers from the forum and historical commentaries in a special report distributed to all members, Ethics and Archaeology: Challenges for the 1990s, edited by Mark. J. Lynott and Alison Wylie (1995). Member comments were solicited in this special report, through a notice in SAA Bulletin, and at two sessions held at the SAA booth during the 1995 annual meeting in Minneapolis. The final principles, presented here, are revised from the original draft based on comments from members and the Executive Board.

Principle No. 7:
Records and Preservation
Archaeologists should work actively for the preservation of, and long term access to, archaeological collections, records, and reports. To this end, they should encourage colleagues, students, and others to make responsible use of collections, records, and reports in their research as one means of preserving the in situ archaeological record, and of increasing the care and attention given to that portion of the archaeological record which has been removed and incorporated into archaeological collections, records, and reports.

Survey Ethics

As a general, a survey should:

- Practice point recording by means that meet acceptable standards in American archaeology
- Avoid any conflicts with Native American beliefs, rights, and tribal laws.
- Report to state agencies any observations of site looting, destruction, or vandalism.
- Comply and help enforce state burial laws.
- Publish all observations and gained knowledge on state cultural resources.
- Avoid any circumstances that place monetary values on antiquities.
- Ensure that all survey data are in the public realm.
- Provide certified and/or highly experienced analysis for paleopoint recording.
- Encourage point owners to participate in public archaeology.
- Ensure that all data collecting and storage meets basic scientific methodologies.
- Maintain databases so that they a compatible with computer industry standards.
- Always assume that all archaeology is public archaeology.

Part Two – Basic Modeling for Surveys

Model Organization

Figure 11 provides the high-level architectural framework for this model which is broken down into views. Each view cell (called a node) in the model has a title, and its affected inputs, outputs, controls, and constraints. Occasionally, a node contains an output constraint, such as Best Practices, as shown in the example. This framework shows the inputs, controls, constraints, and outputs as they apply to the McCary Survey. They may vary in other surveys, but they generally offer the philosophy of a survey operation. These factors are further defined, illustrated, and discussed in the following paragraphs.

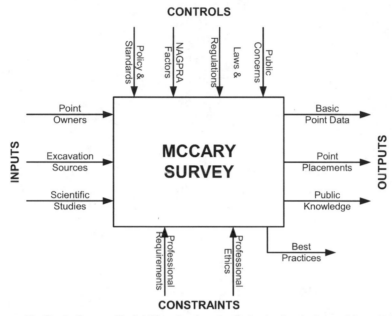

Figure 11 - Basic Survey Model Showing Inputs, Outputs, Controls, and Constraints

The model unit nodes, which reflect specific activities or processes in a survey, are:

N0 – Survey Model
N1 – Logic Flow of the Survey
N2 – Dataflow in a Survey
N3 – Artifact Flow in a Survey
N4 – Operational Flow in a Survey
N5 – Analytical Process in a Survey
N6 – Process Control in a Survey.

Figure 12 shows the relationships of these nodes, and Table 5 provides the basic operationalization for each node. All nodes are controlled by written, in place, procedures, policies, and standards for the survey. All these documents can be grouped into a single document, such as Survey Operating Principles. But nonetheless, they should be written and open to public access and inspection. As suggested, the survey is a public realm operation for the advancement of science – and the study of Paleoindians. This model provides the structure for this study. Additionally, the McCary Survey procedures are provided in Hranicky and Johnson (2005) and located at: www.mccary-survey.com.

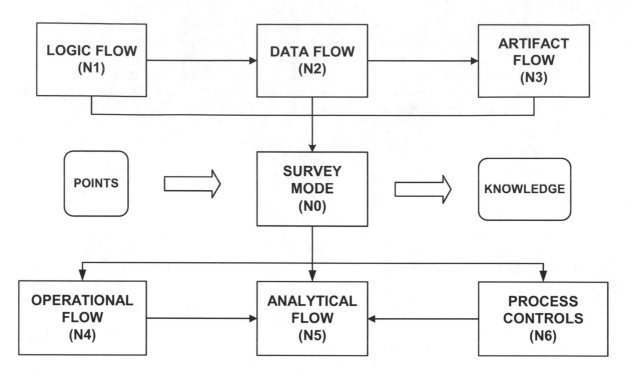

Figure 12 – Survey Model Showing All Nodes

Nodes:

Node (N0) – Survey Mode
Node (N1) – Logic Flow
Node (N2) – Data Flow
Node (N3) – Artifact Flow
Node (N4) – Operational Flow
Node (N5) – Analytical Flow
Node (N6) – Process Controls

For definitions, see Table 5.

Table 5 – Survey Model Nodes					
Node	Input	Output	Control	Constraint	Function
N0 – Survey Model					
N1 – Logic Flow of the Survey	Point records	Public records Survey reports	State boundaries Legal point ownership	Point owner Lithic material Point properties	Provides a systematic collection of data
N2 – Dataflow in a survey	Electronic recording Pencil recording	Webpage Paper publications Population data Electronic database National database	Data validation Processing methods	Requirements Standards Survey processes	Provides methods and practices for initial-to-database recording
N3 – Artifact Flow in a Survey	Legal point discovery	Relic world Destroyed Museum	Public lands Indian lands Indian rights Ethics Deed of gift Bill of sale	Point source Point supply Legal rights Market values	Provides a view of a general history of a Clovis point
N4 – Operational Flow in a Survey	Point find and location data	Point placement in private/public repository Publication of the point	Transportation Laboratory	Ownership Analysis methods Validation & verification methods Storage	Provides the procedures for turning collection data into point information
N5 – Analytical Process in a Survey	Survey form	Knowledge database in archaeology	Measurements Scientific methods Professionalism	Chronology Geography Environment Settlement	Provides the basic processes and procedures for analyzing a point
N6 – Process Control in a Survey	Survey practices	Clovis publications	Indian rights Ethical practices	Methods Standards Area coverage Science	Provides the philosophy of the survey

Basic Model Operations

Using this model as an example, a survey can operate as an independent program whose basic goals are to record (and validate) all new/old found paleopoints found in its geographic area of responsibility.[20] Generally, a survey has a director, database administrator, and a publication specialist, who are usually rolled up into one person. The point is always the input and initializes the recording process. Naturally, some form of data storage is required. The output is always the publication and allowing access to the survey's database. With the advent of Webpages, record access is easier and opens *the door* for scholarly access. The general public also has the opportunity to browse the survey's records.

Recording points is a one-on-one operation, namely recording individual point traits and making measurements. Whereas, a survey is a collection of traits and contributes them to attributes of a class or type, in this case Clovis and other paleopoints. Traits are always variables, but still conform to a parsimonious way (fewest dimensional variations) of a type. A Clovis point has landmarks which make it a member of a type. Landmarks are based on benchmarks in a collective database.

Landmark – specific variables needed to define a point in a type. Landmarks are assumed to be related to tool function and purpose. For points, it is a reference to major parts, especially attributes which are common to all points, which includes: point tip, medial axis, blade edge, shoulder, base, and for all points, notch (indentation), and stem. Within landmarks, traits are allowed as variations on attributes.

Benchmark – analytical reference which may be an estimate or count from which a population measurement can be made. It is based on measurements from a specific landmark on points. As an analytical tool, it is a system of establishing tool class and/or industry frequencies within a river drainage, county, state, region, or national area. Once a benchmark is established, any site material can be compared to it. Traits are not allowed in benchmarks.

Landmark versus Benchmark – landmark is the functional/positional attribute needed to define a tool. Whereas, benchmark is the numeric evaluation of a functional attribute on the tool that is needed to classify or type it.

Recording a point's data is an empirical process based on (controlled by) the point's properties. Like traits, these point properties have variation, but are limited to the scope of "What would be called Clovis." Landmarks and benchmarks can easily be incorporated into standards and training survey recorders to observe them empirically. When used in analyses, benchmarks and landmarks tend to be observations for physical properties that are either present or absent on the point.

The initializing event for the survey is a request to enter a point in the survey. A survey data collection form is used. See Appendix E for a survey form example. All data entries match fields in the database. This form can be completed by hand or data can be entered directly into a PC which is used to transfer the record to the database. Continuous review ensures that newly-recorded data are not lost. Also, a technical review is performed early in the recording process, which may reject the point. The survey must set policies as to what level and kind of missing data are acceptable. Tentative point number assignment is not recommended; the point is either acceptable with

---

[20] Paleopoint is used for the basic term in recording artifacts; a survey should be oriented towards a specific point classification.

complete data or it is not and must be recorded at another time. Figure 13 provides the basic recording proves for a survey.

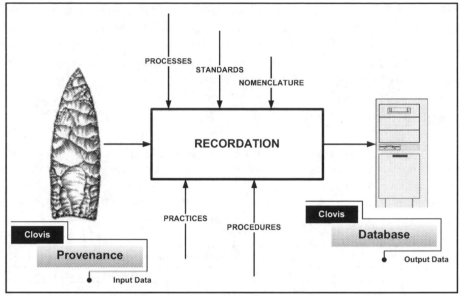

Figure 13 – The Clovis Recording Process

Inputs and Outputs

The basic model operates on two physical operations, which are:

- Inputs
- Outputs.

<u>Inputs</u> are the initializing operation on which the survey processes a point. Input can be data transfer from written documents or by electronic inputs from scanners or other digital equipment. Generally or traditionally, data are input from the survey form.

<u>Outputs</u> are the finalizing operation on which the survey generates from its processing. Output can be in the form of paper reports or digital files and tables.

Constraints and Controls

This model provides the means to classify and coordinate (incorporate) factors which affect the survey. While most are not officially part of a survey, they do "regulate" the survey's operation so that its credibility remains unquestioned. They are grouped as:

- Constraints
- Controls.

<u>Constraints</u> on the survey are federal/state legal obligations and ethical practices for controlling and accessing the database. Constraints are basically technological, but user information availability, as mentioned, is a factor. They are factors that are usually outside of the survey's operation. The model contains numerous constraints in the acquisition of paleopoint data that must be incorporated in the survey's processes. As especially noted, the survey should maintain written procedures,

53

policies, and practices which include point verification and validation methods for handling constraints (Figure 14).

Controls, like constraints, affect the survey's operation. The controls are the data validation methods and general processing methods. There are restrictions that are identified and incorporated into the survey's written procedures, practices, policies, and standards for complying with controls. They are based on or taken from the professional archaeological community, but also conform to factors, such as Native American concerns and rights.

Model Regulations

Paperwork, now computerwork, is a way of the so-called modern world. A successful survey is one that has proven regulations for its operation. They provide consistency and continuous credibility for the survey. These regulations are used to cite reason, ethics, and general operations of the survey for the public and the scientific community. Table 6 provides restrictions on the survey which should be incorporated in the survey's documents.

| Table 6 – Written Survey Regulations ||
Survey Restriction	Survey Documents
Controls	Processes Standards
Constraints	Practices Procedures

Survey Operating Documents

The basic survey documents[21] are:

▶ **Processes** – a set of operational methods for studying paleopoints.

▶ **Standards** – a set of terms, concepts, and measurements for studying paleopoints.

▶ **Practices** – a set of activities on studying paleopoints; includes ethics.

▶ **Procedures** – a set of physical (scientific) ways of recording paleopoints.

Basic Survey Operations

This model presents general practices for operation (Figure 11). The survey is basically:

- Recordkeeping
- Database management
- And, publications.

---

[21] As discussed in text, lessons learned, database evaluation, and best practice documents should be maintained by a survey.

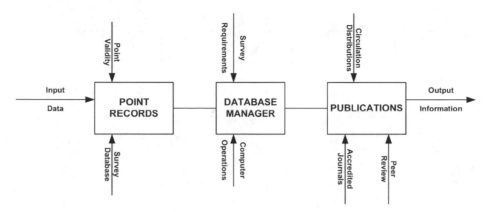

Figure 14 – Basic Survey Operations

For practical as well as scientific reasons, there should be only one survey in a state. And, the survey should have a review process for accepting and numbering points. For example, North Carolina has two surveys; a duplication of effort? Pennsylvania has an open survey where anyone can contribute a point for inclusion in the survey; credibility of the survey's database? And, the survey needs sanctioning from a state's archaeological community; survey legitimacy recognition? A basic requirement for the survey: the owner of a submitted point **must** allow its publication.

Survey Host

The survey should remain independent from state/federal agencies because of possible conflicts of interest that may arise during the survey's operation. Academic and state archaeological societies make ideal candidates for hosting or ownership of the survey. While all survey data should be part of the public domain, the survey itself must be protected, such as intellectual property rights, copyrights for artwork, and general operations protections. Basically, the survey should be incorporated in the state where it resides. By issuing corporate shares, the survey can easily have host-to-host and director-to-director transfers – simply by vote. The corporation should be nonprofit, and all labor should be voluntary.

Model Overview

Regardless of its methodologies, the success of a survey depends on its contributors who come forward with their private finds or archaeologically-sourced finds. With a reasonable caution, a survey depends on the artifact collectors and cooperation from professional archaeologists excavating Paleoindian sites. Both are the primary sources for point submissions. This survey model shows the factors and processes that comprise a survey's operation. As mentioned, survey constraints and controls are identified. All of these elements are discussed throughout the publication. Figure 15 provides a survey structure for physical operations, all of which are needed for a successful survey.

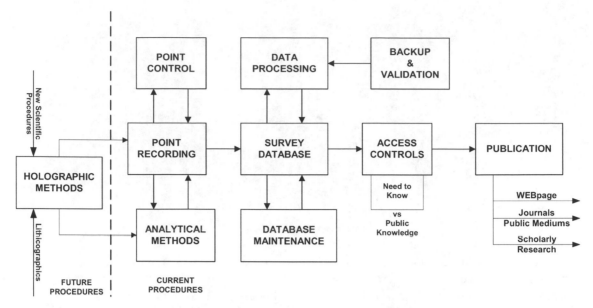

Figure 15 - Survey Model Overview (N0 Node)

Point recording is the primary focus of a survey and is essentially a short-term activity. But in terms of the total survey operation, recordation produces long-term point record maintenance, all of which lead to publications and additions to the archaeological database. Access to the survey database is generally free; however, due to hackers and other misfits on the Internet, access to the database should be limited to recognized scholars and sincere amateur archaeologists. Always back up survey databases with several copies which have been scanned with a virus checking software. Holographic methods are shown in the model. It will be a method of scanning a point to obtain its metrics, morphology, and lithic composition – a future of point recording.

Mechanics of the Model

This model is a combination of data flow and survey process models that offer a total operation of a fluted point survey. It is based on the McCary Fluted Point Survey®, which the author operates. This survey has over 50 years of contribution to the study of Virginia Paleoindian prehistory and has delivered 1000+ points to the archaeological world. McCary (1951) launched both the Williamson Paleoindian site and his survey in his classic workshop publication in American Antiquity. He started the Survey which was later named after him, and it is the oldest survey in the U.S.

The model operates with two approaches in the acquisition of point data. They are:

- First hand recording either in the field or in the laboratory
- Holographic recording either remotely or in the laboratory.

First hand recording is what most surveys will use; it is a one-on-one with the point's owner. Futuristically, holographic recording involves setting up recording equipment, such as cameras, graphic software, and computers; it is purely a mechanical method that does not involve the human interface. Hranicky and Johnson (2005) discuss point recording methodologies and Appendix B has procedures for recording points. From this, the model operates in the form of a logic flow (data collection) and then it follows a data flow (mechanics of data storage and movement). Next, the model has a processing phase for collections and research investigations.

56

Logic Flow

The basic operation of a survey is a process of collecting the biography of a point, including its owner. This is often an oral history of the point and probably does not offer a specific provenance. Next is collecting the morphological properties of the point, which are entered into a survey database. Figure 16 shows the basics of a survey operation. Logic of the survey recording process follows established scientific methods. The flow is from input data to output information. Logic is essentially the professional philosophy that controls and organizes survey data and files.

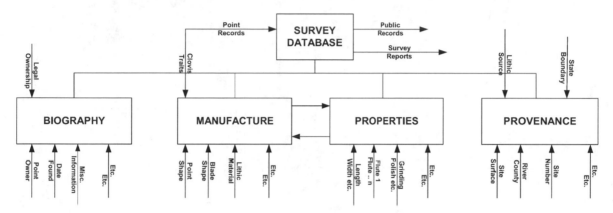

Figure 16 – Logic Flow of a Survey Operation (N1 Node)

Data Flow

Data flow is a process that is based on the survey's written procedures. There must be a process from collecting data to maintaining the survey's database. Figure 17 shows a typical process. For best practices, all survey points and data should be reviewed by a survey committee.

Data flow is the movement of initial data to some form of a collective output – or, an output that produces information. It parallels logic flow. The final location for data is, of course, the survey's database and, perhaps, display windows on the Internet. A basic component of data flow is to determine and ensure data validity. Data validation is determined by following the survey's policies and procedures – and compliance to sound archaeological practices and data collection methods. For contemporary archaeology, data flow means electronic capturing and processing of selected, relevant data.

57

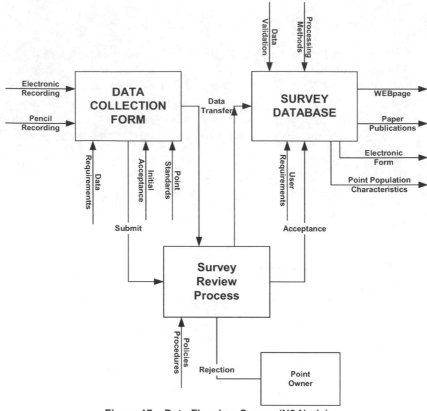

Figure 17 – Data Flow in a Survey (N2 Node)

Survey as a Process

The survey offers a single-source investigation of Paleoindian points. And, it offers a coordinated effort within the archaeological community. Most members of this community are constantly searching for point owners and encouraging participation in recording paleopoints. The survey can be viewed as a credible activity for "chasing down" paleopoints and getting them recorded. This process often leads to the public informing the archaeological community of new sites. A survey often drives the process of investigating and researching paleopoints. Additionally, most surveys monitor the hands-to-hands flow (exchange) of Paleoindian points in the relic/collector world.

Perhaps as part of the survey's governance, it should actively pursue a role of encouraging point owners to place their points into the public realm, namely public museums. As should be noted, all point owners are simply temporary custodians, and when they die, someone else carries the burden of privately owning the points. As in:

> **Disposal of private/public collections through sale, trade, public placement, or research activities is solely the concern for the advancement of the archaeology's mission to safeguard antiquities.**

For the present, archaeology relies on the Society for American Archaeology (SAA), state archaeological agencies, and state archaeological society members to monitor all these consequences for artifacts and sites – this seems to be a losing battle…

Survey Model Operations

The real justification for the survey is that the point contributes to archaeology's knowledge base. If for no other reason, the director of a survey should be a professional prehistoric archaeologist. This person would have the training and experience that is needed to support data acquisition as a public policy and avoid contributing to the relic underworld. Professional analytical skills and methods are a basic requirement; this is not to say that advanced amateurs cannot develop these skills and learn professional practices. Also, it is true that to get to and record valid paleopoints, the survey staff must participate and probably be an accepted member of the antiquity-oriented world of collectors.

Figure 18 shows the basic movement of most American artifacts including Paleoindian points. A survey becomes involved in the flow if the point is submitted for recording. If not, the survey has a second chance if the point eventually becomes the property of a public agency, institution, or museum. A problem for most surveys is a Native point found in a neighboring state which somehow transforms its find provenance to the host-survey's provenance. Obviously, points found on or near another state's boundaries might be justified as an inclusion in the survey. These are called and recorded as border points. This provenance-moving is especially a problem for surveys that do not have counter-partners in neighboring states.

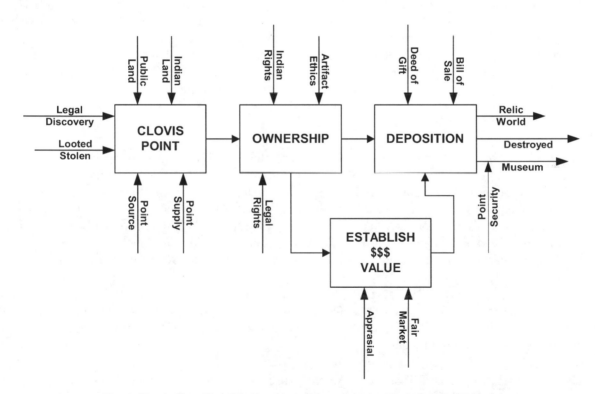

Figure 18 – Artifact Flow (Modern Circumstances of the Clovis Point) (N3 Node)

At this place in this publication, and at horror to some archaeologists, all paleopoints have two types of value: 1) monetary and 2) knowledge. A survey must deal with both values. Essentially, the survey promotes the public good rather than individual financial gains. Any time a paleopoint is added to a survey, its monetary value is greatly increased. And, the survey authenticates the artifact, all of which invite the relic world to participate in survey requests. Surveys should avoid getting into point appraisals and outright purchases, but the nature of the relic (nonarchaeological) world, namely museums and state agencies, sometimes requires expert advice and appraisals for which the survey is an ideal candidate. This is a consequence that is necessary for the public domain of Native American materials; not *all* will agree.

This value factor is *really* difficult to separate the *rocks* from the scientists. Clovis points are tools that served life times in the past; they were discarded when expended by Early Americans. Today, they are samples of prehistoric life times; they are only rocks that contain cultural information. They are not rocks having dollar signs attached to them. But for most, they cannot make the distinction between historic and monetary values. A few-too-many archaeologists see first the monetary values in their Paleoindian acquisitions, then settle down for serious ... whatevers. There is no dollar value on knowledge; and, more importantly, all knowledge must be part of the public domain. This is truly what separates collectors (and some amateurs) from professional archaeologists. Then again, bring up Clovis points at any meeting, especially their movement in the nonpublic world of antiquities, and "sit back" for a lively discussion.[22]

The survey process can be a disaster for a state's inventory of Clovis points and records, as its director usually plays a role in point movement and usually influences the placement of points. Most Clovis points are single, occasional finds by people who do not have a direct role in the archaeology of a state. They come to or are referred to the survey director to assist them with finding out what they have, and most important to them, what is the value of the point. Here, reference is made to the point's historic value, but, in some cases, the director has the persuasiveness to acquire the point. Over the years, the director can build a massive Clovis collection. As a recent case in this argument, the survey's director dies leaving the collection to heirs who sell it, often for *big bucks*. This leaves a void in state collections that can never be justified by the survey. A survey has a moral and ethical requirement to perform recordation in a scientific manner and without personal interest or accessions. Personal collecting has **no** place in the operation of a survey – never.

The survey's world is controlled by: 1) the points that are found, such as on public or private lands,[23] 2) Native American rights, 3) legal exchanges of artifacts, 4) deeds of gift or bill of sales, and 5) numerous activities outside archaeology. The major control is the supply and availability of points and, of course, market values. As with any high-value item, security is a major concern. For survey, point transportation for recording is best accomplished by hand-to-hand exchanges or, minimally, with insured public carriers. A survey should provide cautions and suggest security practices for point owners. In some cases, owners are unaware of the security problem.

The recording process involves completing a survey point form. An example is presented in Appendix E. Once the data have been collected, point images, photographs, drawings, and rubbings are created. Appendix G shows examples and Hranicky and Johnson (2005) provide an overview of the entire point recoding process.

The analytical process is difficult to present because of its lengthy methodologies and procedures used to analyze points. The principal concerns are to study the point's manufacture, lithic source, environmental situation, context and chronology, and provenance (Figure 19). Most surveys divide point recording into field and laboratory sources. Field collection is recording the point at the

---

[22] The author participated in SAA (Denver 2002) panel discussion entitled Exploring Links between Site Destruction and Commercial Markets in Archaeological Materials, chaired by Julie Zimmer and Alex Barker.
[23] Points found on state/federal lands constitute a concern that must be addressed in the survey's policy document. At no time or place should anyone collect on these lands. Permits are required and only for professional archaeological investigations.

owner's premises; whereas, laboratory recording is, obviously, the preferred method. While in the laboratory, the point can undergo nondestructive testing, such as patination analysis, refractive indexing, specific gravity analysis, organic residue analyses, or lithic identification; testing is generally an observational approach for recording point properties. Observations are based on experimental archaeology data and information. Comparative data learned for Native points also bring into play observations that are needed to analyze a point. Analysis is applied to landmark and benchmark data.

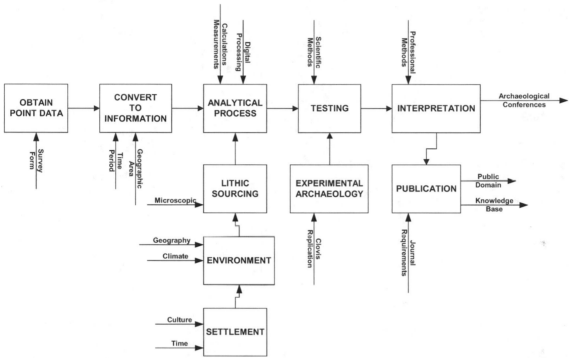

Figure 19 – Analytical Process (All Components of the Technical View) (N4 Node)

The process flow is a system orientation that examines the entire recording process (Figure 20). It includes point origins (modern discovery), finder credibility, mechanics of recording the point, entering data, processing data, concern over the point's home, and finally, publication. Each of these categories could be discussed separately, but these would vary from survey to survey, and there is no generic definition and description for them. Controls are getting the point, measuring it, recording its properties, and ensuring that it is properly curated. The point's publication is a *given* for any survey. Constraints are found in learning the point's modern ancestry, such as was it found on public land, does the owner have title to it, and then database restrictions, such as size, images, etc. This is the most volatile aspect in a survey operation. Point credibility, ownership, provenance, and attributes are all basic complicating considerations; a point data integration – there are no easy means to approach these factors.

61

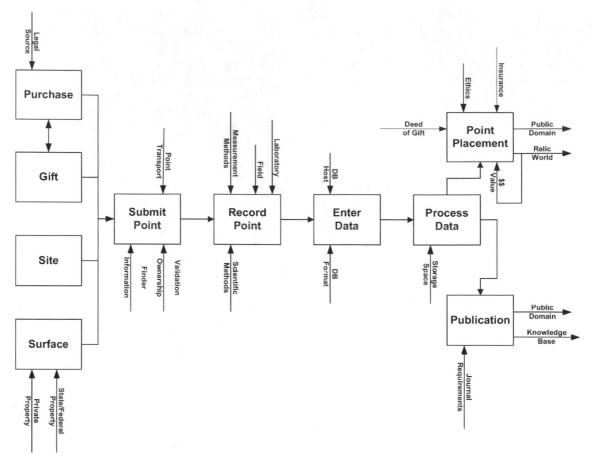

Figure 20 – Process (Operational) Flow (Procedures for Turning Data into Information) (N5 Node)

Survey Database

Recording points requires a computer-based form of recordkeeping. Most contract firms, state/federal agencies, and colleges/institutions have database managers who perform these duties for their operations. However, survey archaeologists should be aware of and use the techniques and practices so that research designs and investigations conform to established policies and procedures within the general academic community of archaeology. The standard recommended here is: ANSI/ISO standard. As for software, Microsoft's Excel and Access are common database programs. However, for large databases, a higher level of software is required. A sample database is presented in Appendix D.

Regardless of the recordkeeping techniques, file and record maintenance is the key to a successfully-operated survey (Figure 21). It involves all forms, e.g., narrative, graphic, data, computers, or information in permanent form so that it can be retrieved, reproduced, and most importantly, preserved. The constraints on the survey process are standards and policies, archaeological and scientific methods, and public cooperation. For an example, see Hranicky and Johnson (2005). These factors are discussed throughout this publication.

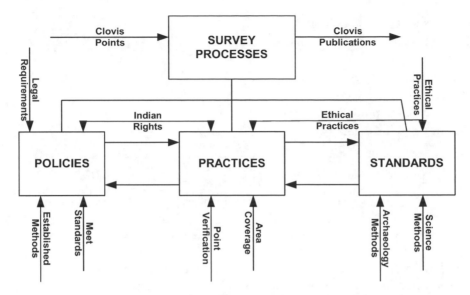

Figure 21 – Process Controls in a Survey (N6 Node)

The survey database is composed of point records that are based on the data collection form. Data from the form are transferred into the database, either manually or electronically. As a suggestion, a four-table, relational database should be maintained; but for small surveys, a single table can be used. These tables could be: point data, ownership, current locations, and graphics.[24] The basic output is the survey report which can be printed after each record (or group of records) is entered. Reports are also generated in electric forms, such as CDs and Internet displays. No calculation fields should be stored in the database. They waste space and can be calculated in report printing, statistical studies, or window displays. Each point represents a single record.

Survey Outputs

A survey should make its data available in numerous medias, such as paper reports, webpages, and CDs. A major contribution is to provide a state map with county point distributions. Another form of an output is teaming with a state archaeological society and participating in its activities. Based on the survey population, it can output benchmark and landmark requirements and specifications. With graphic and gaming softwares, output can be in the form of hypothetical point entities that are based on user queries.

Survey Presentations

Types of survey presentations are only limited by the user's ability to create them. Presentations can be programmed or manually created; all of which represent the survey's contribution to the archaeology's knowledge base. The database structure can be manipulated by an inference system (software) and pattern-matching techniques (queries) to answer questions, draw conclusions, or otherwise perform intelligent operations (Figure 22). Some of the operations are:

- Propositional logic
- Predicate calculus

---

[24] For both point faces, point images, rubbings, and drawings require massive amounts of computer storage space. And, daily maintenance, such as backups, is required.

- Create scripts for modeling
- Create lists for research comparisons
- Design decision tables
- Create decision trees
- Produce knowledge maps
- Produce geographic distributions
- Produce graphic displays.

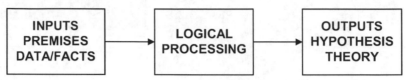

Figure 22 – Survey Presentation Process

The model views presented here are knowledge parts that are composed of nodes (links) that show a hierarchical or relational connection among its objects and their data. One factor that has not been mentioned is: the survey can show inheritance for its data. For example, data collected by various survey directors or data imported from other sources. For the present, the McCary Survey is a sole-source for its data. Also, the database can be manipulated to borrow characteristics or properties from other points, within or outside the current database.

Probably, the immediate future for survey is to create hypertexts and web-based database presentations. These are visual presentations, but can be combined with the *ole fashioned* paper-copy reports.

Model Views

When surveys are operated archaeologically and within practical capabilities of modern science, data recovery and recording provides a tremendous amount of insight to the point's history. As science finds its new inventions, innovations, and perfecting current technologies, the analysis of paleopoints has an endless range of methods for acquiring more, never-known information about the past. New methods, or at least taking advantage of science's apparatus of knowledge gathering, involve techniques, such as lithocrystallography, index refractions, microwear residues, patination aging, reduction modeling, stone workability dynamics and scales, electronegativity, lifecycle and breakage algorithms, lithic fingerprinting, and numerous scientific analyses (Hranicky 2004). This survey process can be called a holographic approach which includes a point's demensic measurements, volumlithic calculations, and topographic mapping.

Model views are not currently practiced in the McCary Survey, but it is moving to this model which will become its Operations Manual. As such, an integrated design is not offered; however, it is a future for fluted point surveys. Additionally in modeling there are two basic types: logical and physical (object). Both have high-level applications in prehistoric archaeology.

> **Models are a way to enhance the physical processes governing human behavior with artifacts. And. They generate reliable artifact results (testing) that can be used as benchmarks for artifact type comparisons.**

These views offer a relational model for paleopoints. They are:

- Cultural view
- Technological view
- Systems view.

The <u>cultural view</u> is the governing view for the survey in that it only focuses on the Paleoindian period with a specialty of fluted points. The survey can include nonfluted points, but this complicates survey membership. The survey contributes to this view by making its data available to archaeological investigations and/or museum or educational displays. The survey offers numerical facts about fluted point technology in a given state. It offers iconic and analog data modeling.

The <u>technical view</u> is the heart of the survey. Without technical investigations, point data can become contaminated with false data which, of course, leads to false interpretations about the Paleoindian era in the Americas. This problem is not limited only to the state producing the data, but to other states whose researchers use national Paleoindian data. While the technical view has an output, namely interpretative information, it is subject to operational inputs from the professional community, namely scientific methods and recording techniques. It offers symbolic data and physical property (as in topography) modeling.

The <u>systems view</u> is the integrated study of Paleoindian technology as it was used in prehistory. Collected data provide insights to numerous cultural situations and livelihood viability of early Americans. This view outputs information on cultural processes in Native American history and includes their traditions. It presents the point as a functional entity in a social setting in antiquity. It offers canonical data modeling.

Figure 23 shows these views in conjunction with a basic survey operation, which is producing data/information for archaeology's knowledge base. After which, it places survey efforts and results in the public domain. This aspect cannot be overly emphasized – there is no private archaeology (as in McGimsey 1972). All survey data must be accessible to scholars conducting scientific research.

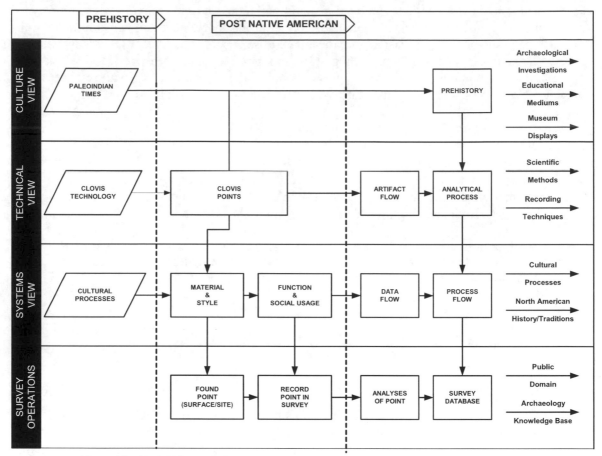

Figure 23 – Model Views (Culture, Technical, and Systems Views) and Survey Operation

Cultural View

The cultural view is the archaeological framework in which the model exists (Figure 24). For the model, technology is used since recordation basically involves the technological aspects of Paleoindian technology. Other concerns do occur, namely economics, politics, sociology, religion, art, and language – the total cultural view. While present in the paleopoint's environment, they are not generally part of the physical world of material culture. These nontechnological factors are often latent conditions in the archaeological record. Of course, they can be noted when observed.

The cultural view is the complex set of knowledge, social conditions, and technologies existing and developed around specific conditions of populations and communities indigenous to a particular geographic area. It refers to knowledge developed by these populations, as well as knowledge developed through interaction with other populations in surrounding areas.

This view focuses on the contrasts, impacts (historical and current) and dynamics of modernity and traditionalism on indigenous knowledge and lifeways. The main focus of the research should be on the delineation of indigenous socio-cultural systems. The cultural view involves:

- Cultural associations is society
- Ethical and political systems
- Habitation and settlement
- Curation of raw materials
- Physical skills/educational systems
- Fauna/flora exploitation
- Cultural change processes
- Religion and ideologies
- Indigenous language(s)
- Traditions/worldviews
- Quality of life factors.

Archaeological interpretations about prehistoric contents and material remains are continuously changing; the basic model structure for Paleoindian history remains as a general portrayal of Early Americans during the formative stage of U.S. history. However, changes do occur, and the survey model must be flexible to accommodate them without corrupting its database. Two factors affect the cultural view, which are the environment and chronological situations of the point being recorded.

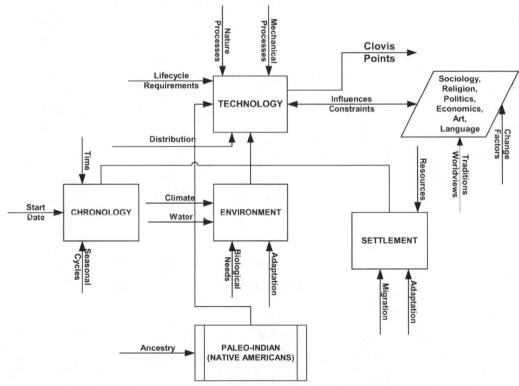

Figure 24 - Culture Overview from a Technology Perspective

As once said somewhere, basic data never changes; the collection of data must be in a manner that allows for new requirements and the expansion of old data. This comes down to the survey data collection form and just what is a comprehensive collection method. For most survey records, there is no second-doing a point recording. The paleopoint population in any state is highly volatile; namely points travel, even today, from hands-to-hands without regard to archaeological principles and ethics. Re-recording of points from early days of the survey is one method of ensuring data validation and integrity. A sample survey form is presented in Appendix E.

Technical View

The technical view for most archaeologists is the part of prehistory that offers the basic romance of archaeology, namely the study of the Paleoindian point's physical properties as in topography or morphology. The flow of a paleopoint analysis is the principal control of a survey's technological expertise. Without a technical evaluation at all stages of recording a point, recording failures, misinterpretation, and/or false documents can become part of the survey's database.

The technical view involves:

- Raw materials
- Curation practices
- Toolmaking methods
- Skills
- Tool usage.

A paleopoint-based standard for a survey's analytical process provides consistency in recording traits and attributes (its entity composition). However, the paleopoint standard should be based on regional, if not national, traits as opposed to national attributes. Traits as well as attribute frequencies have a wide-range of variables. Thus, this standard should be comprehensive, but flexible in usage. Also, various styles have been proposed for paleopoints, for example Kraft (1973), McCary (1975), and Justice (1985); the survey's standards document should cover this topic, as it is a major concern in determining what and how points get recorded. Pointmaking skill is a major factor in prehistory. Various skill levels are probably major factors in type variation in archaeology. See Appendix J.

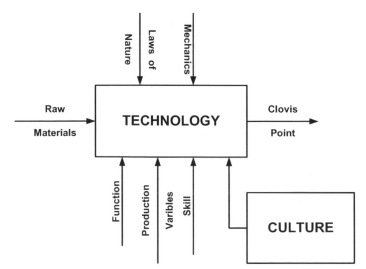

Figure 25 - A Clovis Technology/Culture Model

68

Attributes make up a type and are generic qualities for all points in that type. On the other hand, traits are point specific and can vary regionally within a type. A survey is basically recording traits as opposed to attributes (Figure 25).

As the technical view would imply, Figure 26 shows the input/output controls and constraints for a Clovis point. For the technical view of the point, culture is the controlling factor. Natural processes in Nature are the constraints. A successfully manufactured point is a tool output for this view.

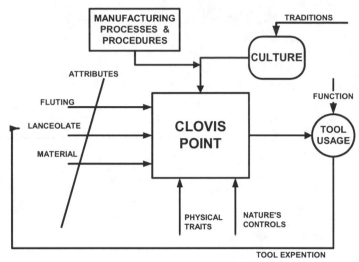

Figure 26 – A Clovis Point View

Systems View

The systems view is the most difficult of the views to construct. It should always be defined as:

- Open system which has new or continuous inputs and outputs (dynamic processes)
- Closed system which is fixed as in a historical context (now processes are static).

System

For lithic tool production and usage, it is any combination of activities, events, quantities, properties, and attributes that, when considered as a collective whole, are representative of a single entity. All systems are subdividable and for lithic technology always represent space and time. For prehistory, all systems (prob ψ) can only be described as a probability (<1).

Systems Thinking

A method of formal analysis in which the object of study is viewed as comprising distinct analytical subunits. Thus in archaeology, it comprises a form of explanation in which a society or culture is seen through the interaction and interdependence of its component parts; these are referred to as system parameters, and may include such things as population size, settlement pattern, crop production, technology etc.

Defining a System

The definition of a system is much more difficult than definitions in the technology and culture views. Based on General Systems Theory, systems are:

1 - A view for the ensemble of interaction parts, the sum of which exhibits behavior not localized in its constituent parts. That is, "the whole is more than the sum of the parts."

2 - Views which can be physical, biological, social, or symbolic; or it can be comprised of one or more of these.

3 - Change which is seen as a transformation of the system in time, which, nevertheless, conserves its identity within the view. Growth, steady state, and decay are major types of change.

4 - Goal-directed behavior which characterizes the changes observed in the state of the system view. A system is seen to be actively organized in terms of the goal and, hence, can be understood to exhibit "reverse causality."

5 – View has "Feedback" which is the mechanism that mediates between the goal and system behavior in the system.

6 - Time which is a central variable in system theory. This view provides a referent for the very idea of dynamics. Systems are not static.

7 - The "boundary" which serves to delineate the system from the environment and any subsystems from the system as a whole, as system views show boundaries.

8 - System-environment interactions which can be defined as the input and output of matter (properties), information (data), and energy. The system can be open, closed, or semipermeable to the host environment.

The Systems View

The systems (or historic) view involves paleopoint usage in social settings and their governing properties that create the variations in type attributes. It involves a data and process flow for point operations and functions within a social unit (Figure 27). While similar to a cultural analysis, systems are part of intercultural processes that may simply be called universal, such as manufacturing tools to building shelters. It is a view of interconnected activities where tools play (usually) minor roles in a society.

The systems view involves:

- Adaptation to environments
- Functional tool usage for work
- Traditional histories
- Social organization affecting tools.

As used in the survey model, it is an organized co-ordination of resources, procedures and standards, and policies needed to record prehistoric activities, namely Paleoindian pointmaking and its cultural systems that influenced point production. A systems approach for the survey parallels the prehistoric culture systems and offers a totality view of Paleoindians. This view has two constraint outputs: an electronic file and a dataset that reflects the basic characteristics of the state fluted point population. The latter output indicates some type of cultural system is present during the Paleoindian era.

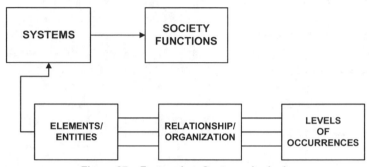

Figure 27 – Factors in a Systems Analysis

Paleopoint technology, namely Clovis, is a closed system that existed in a specific time period; in this case, the Paleoindian era. Even though closed, this system exerted influences on other forms of prehistoric technology and provides a legacy technology which continues through the Woodland period. As a definition of a Paleoindian system, it is:

1 – Technology as a coherent system that was organized and transferred from social group to group.

2 – Culture that was the controlling mechanism which maintained its coherence, namely point redundancy.

3 – Social boundaries that are delineated by systems inputs and outputs, influenced by environments, and regulated by raw materials.

4 – A system that was operational, purposive, and had the following:

- Natural systems
- Human activity systems
- Socio-political systems
- Ideological systems.

5 – Systems that are predictive and contain problem-solving solutions for survival.

6 – Systems that change with time and technology. Paleoindian technology was subject to change agents, such as population pressures, raw material availability, and environmental pressures.

7 – Systems represent adaptive strategies which were probably environmentally determined or at least were influenced.

8 – Technology was based on legacy forms in pre-Clovis eras.

Using Model Views

The above model views do not operate independently; they are interrelated and, in some cases, difficult to isolate, for example, a technological presentation of fluted points. Collectively, these views represent a knowledge-base with varying degrees of completeness. Central to completeness is the knowledge model, which presents the views (culture, technological, and systems) as problem-solving or topic identification instead of simple representation of facts, such as a table or graph. Problem-solving is a broad category, including what-ifs, cause/effect, evolution, social adoption, change processes, and numerous other usages (Figure 28).

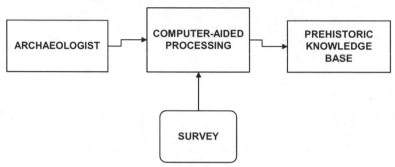

Figure 28 – Using Model Views

These views are ideal for graphic modeling that provides numerous research possibilities and paleopoint interpretative displays, such as:

- As-built graphics
- Reverse engineering graphics
- Expention and wearout graphics
- Human interface graphics.

Tool Model and Simulation Example

The appearance of the everyday world is influenced by many factors, such as shape, color, texture, reflection properties and the surrounding environment. The causes of appearance have long been studied by computer scientists, but not studied generally by archaeologists, but of interest to almost anyone. Recently, modeling and simulating appearance have been studied by anthropologists in computer graphics and computer vision. By modeling the appearance of objects and materials, we are able to render virtual versions of those objects.[25] By measuring appearance, we are able to digitize real world objects and place them in new synthetic environments. Measurement techniques also allow us to experimentally validate different appearance models; in this case, graphical presentations of artifacts. In archaeological graphics (computer visions), artifact structure/function and reflection models can be used to recognize scenes and objects in display images. The following is a brief example of tool modeling and simulation.[26]

A **Tool** is a manually operated implement designed to perform work in order to accomplish a task; facilitating work. It has a natural set of controls and constraints which are manifested in appearance (structure) and its operation (function). This appearance is composed of physical properties which respond to events, which can vary from different human processes; however, each tool property performs a unique set of actions (methods). Method is always restricted to tool properties; thus, multifunctional tools are theoretically impossible, especially for simulation.

If a simulation is set up that initializes a toolmaking process, it would involve one of these methods:

1 – Pecking and grinding
2 – Percussion flaking
3 – Pressure flaking
4 – Striking blades.

Figure 29 shows the basic breakdown for tool production. Graphics would show these stages, of course, depending on the type of tool in the simulation. This is a structural model from which numerous algorithms would be written to perform graphic displays.

---

[25] IBM's new DB2 tools allow users to mix and match patterns and data with native relational data which is stored in native XML. This topic is too advanced for this publication.

[26] Graphical archaeology involves: Boolean operations, kinematics, contouring, digitizing, dithering, object-oriented graphics, surface mapping (topography), animation, BSP trees, ray tracing, Java programming, and numerous methods and techniques which cannot be presented in this brief model. An excellent source is to join the Computer Graphics Society (CGS) and the IEEE Computer Society. Aukstakalis and Blatner (1992), Angel 92002), and Foley and van Dam (1990) are excellent startup publications.

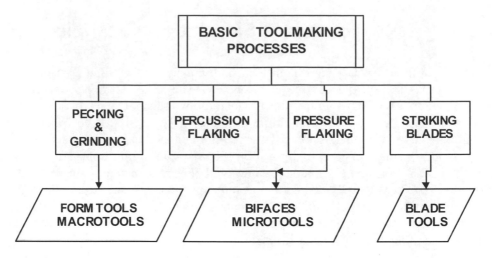

Figure 29 – Basic Toolmaking Process

Tool (Environment, Motion, and Change) - these three factors are the bases for tool analyses and are presented here as basic concepts in graphical archaeology (Figure 30). There are scientific apparatus for assisting analysis, as well as routine archaeological methods, but for basic procedures and techniques all tools can be analyzed and graphically presented by:

1 – Environment
2 – Change
3 – Motion.

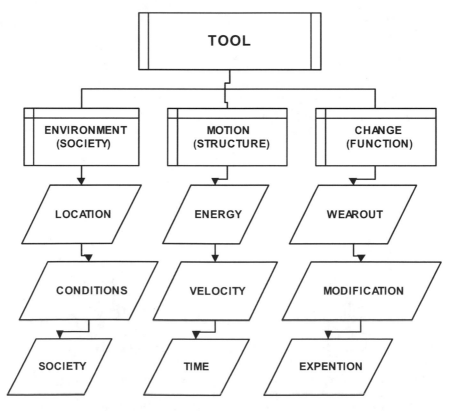

Figure 30 - Tool Concepts: Environment, Motion, and Change

➤ Concept of the Environment

For technology, an environment is a physical collection of attributes and structures that form a system (entity). The environment is the physical space and time in which some entity is found. It is not a stationary system and change is subject to time and the processes (behavior) from within and outside that environment.

All entities have existence in some type of environment, both past and present. All environments have physical boundaries; thus, a structure. Structure is not always completely observable, but it has variables which are usually testable – then replicable. Structural variables are related or connected to the environment (hypothetically). The environment has all properties of a physical object, but at the same time, numerous properties are not necessarily observable, namely pre-Contact cultural factors like structure for a specific function.

One factor that may forever escape archaeology is the cognitive environment that no longer exists, a mythological history of an entity. Additionally, all environments have processes, again which may not be observable analytically. Probably, all environments have actions which affect culture which would modify entity properties and motions. Because of these factors, environment is treated as a constant in graphical archaeology. These following rules usually apply to the concept:

1 – Environment is specified for a single particular system

2 – Environment can affect the system and the system can affect the environment

3 – Constant environment will neither change the system nor will a stable system change the environment

4 – All environments are not stationary and have static processes

5 – All environments have dynamic processes.

➤ Motion as a Concept

Motion is the directional movement of an object; nonstationary position of an object. All human societies have a concept of motion. But, it varies tremendously. The human ability to observe and copy motion constitutes an understanding of the physical processes in Nature. How humans react to tool operation, via motion, remains a study for physical anthropology. However for the moment, the concept of motion is treated as being universal.

Motion is a body that is changing its position. It is always presented with respect to another moving link, such as the human arm or bowstring. There are numerous forms of motion, like plane, helical, spherical, and combinations of motions. Explaining tool motions are used to define and categorize tool functions and useabilities. As a basic rule of motion, it is:
> *Motion cannot occur in free space; it must be linked to an object.*

While it is a simple concept, it is the principal factor in the Ways of Nature and constitutes the exchange of all mechanical devices (machines) in prehistory. All motions are static processes. If an object is moving above the earth's surface in both x and y directions simultaneously, the tool is in motion. This movement has the equivalent motions occurring at the same time, which are:

1 – Tool moves in x (horizontal) direction which is its velocity and is assumed to be a constant

2 – Tool moves in y (vertical) direction with a constant downward acceleration of magnitude g = 9.80 m/s^2.

For motion equations, the following mathematical forms of tool movement are examples:

$$X = (V_1 \cos \theta_1)t$$
$$V_y = V_1 \sin \theta_1 - gt$$
$$Y = (V_1 \sin \theta_1)t - (gt^2)/2$$
$$(V^2)_y = (V_1 \sin \theta_1)^2 - 2gy$$

<u>Note</u>: This is an advanced form of graphic archaeological presentations and will not be attempted here.

Motions (types) for tools are:

1 – Micromotion- hand-held tool movement
2 – Macromotion- throwing tool; projectiling.

By using wear patterns and other variables, such as style and material of Native artifacts, tool motion can be determined as in the following actions:

1 – Cutting- uni- or bifacial motion that is parallel to the use direction and vertical to the target material.

2 – Scraping - transverse motion which is direction (away or towards the user).

3 – Chopping - percussive motion where the workend strikes the target material at 90 degrees.

4 – Adzing - percussive motion where the workend strikes the target material at 45 degrees.

5 - Perforating - rotational motion downward (or through) the target material.

6 – Drilling- reversing, rotational motion downward (or through) the target material.

7 – Axing - heavy percussive motion where the workend strikes the target material at any angle.

8 – Celting - light-to-moderate percussive motion where the workend strikes the target material at any angle.

9 – Planing - horizontal motion to remove part of a target.

10 – Splitting - a downward motion to remove thin slices of a target (usually wood).

There are other possible actions, but these are the principal ones for graphic displays.

➡ Change as a Concept

Change is a property of an entity in which at any given moment (status quo) the entity is not the same as it was previously. Change is always time dependent, measured as a derivative of the entity and is measured in integrals. Change does not have to be a physical property, for example, a change in function. Change is also an entity physical position at T_0 (time), and (movement) T_1, etc. are another position, for example, an arrow in flight. Change is always both a dynamic and static process.

For graphical archaeology, no entity remains constant; there is always change. Change is measured as a time/distance variable or measured for physical reductions or expansions. If change is observable, it is theoretically a replacement for an older entity. For tool analysis, change has three dimensions:

1 – Physical reduction in tool size
2 – Wearout of parts of a tool not necessarily affecting size
3 – Effects on target modification.

Change value is assigned by the researcher and theoretically cannot be measured outside the dimensions of time and space. Both properties must be measured in positive numbers. This often leads to change being evolutionary, which is a false analogy. While using time and space, evolution is another dimension of reality that cannot be quantified. The expression *change over time* is used frequently for artifacts, in particular, ceramics. Quite simply, physical nonorganic objects (technology) do not evolve. However, this does not mean that change has no derivative source; it always has a source. This leaves open the so-called random change, which is usually attributed to culture. As such, for technology, change is always a mechanistic process that is dependent on the source of the entity, subject to its environment, and is no longer stationary (motion). Change also occurs outside the tool assembly, namely the consequence of tool performance of a work task. Faithfully for some, they might argue that this is evolution.

A philosophical question is – is change time dependent? Can change be seen in the ethnographic present? And, lastly, did the Native Americans view change as being opposed to or an alteration of traditional objects? Change is not necessarily a modification of morphology. Naturally, differences in morphology over time as viewed archaeologically are assumed to be changes. For the Native American world, a tool in the ethnographic present is not indicative of change; it is simply a normal entity used to perform a contemporary task. How is change presented so as to reflect Native American antiquities?

Summary

The paleopoint survey is perhaps the best example of public participation in scientific archaeology. Without this input, a survey would be impossible.

This model is flexible and is essentially time-tested. It can be applied to any state-wide survey effort. With the large number of paleopoints available on the relic market, surveys have now presented themselves with a major problem – the fake point. Tankersley (2002) in his book – *In Search of Ice Age Americans* – estimates that 80% of all Clovis points in private collections and museums are fakes. This problem contaminates all efforts at scientifically investigating Clovis technology in the Americas. Regardless of the authentication methods, fake points are getting into legitimate collections and paleo-point databases. But with patient recording of credible points, Paleoindian point surveys can still be maintained and continue to contribute to our knowledge of this early American period in history. The survey is a continuation in the pursuit of knowledge about Paleo-Early Americans.

Several states have or have had fluted point surveys, namely North Carolina, Ohio, Tennessee, Georgia, Pennsylvania, and Alabama. Their operations vary, but overall, they do record paleopoints with a high degree of "sincere efforts" and rely on rigorous scientific methodologies. Staff at the National Park Service started collecting survey data from various states and were forming a national data warehouse – this needs to be revived.

For this publication, it offers suggestions as starting requirements for beginning a survey in a state. Use it freely.

McCary states: "The writer makes no claim that he exhausted the observations which can be made on the data given herein. Better qualified students on the Folsom-complex will no doubt be able to draw more interesting and valuable conclusion from the tables provided by this survey."

Ben C. McCary (1947). Folsom Survey, ASV Quarterly Bulletin, Volume 2, Number 1.

APPENDICES

Appendix A - Concepts and Standards These terms, policies, procedures, methods, and analytical standards (Johnson 1993 and updated in Hranicky 2003) and based on Hranicky's (2004) *Encyclopedia of Concepts and Terminology in American Prehistoric Lithic Technology* are used to describe Clovis attributes and properties in the McCary Fluted Point Survey® of Virginia. **Drawing: Oldest Published (1896) Clovis Point in the World**	

Clovis Achievement in Technology – while there is no defined and proven processor to Clovis technology in Virginia, we can assume some type of motivation challenged them to make the high-quality tools (Hranicky 2003). For an analysis, the central focus of this achievement motivation was their need to meet some standard of excellence (Hranicky 1996). While they could have performed a lithic technology to meet the necessary survival conditions, they performed lithic tasks at a higher level than subsequent populations until the Aztec, Hopewell, Adena, etc. people came centuries afterwards. Clovis technology is not considered by the Survey as the ground floor for prehistoric technology in Virginia; however, for practical applications, Clovis technology is the governing factor for the Survey and its principal trait, fluting, is the key to recording Paleoindian points that are found in Virginia.

Survey purpose: record fluted points found in Virginia and provide the Survey database to scholars studying American prehistory. While principally a Clovis point record, any fluted point from the Paleoindian period can be recorded and included in the Survey. The Survey maintains an electronic database of all its recorded points which is available to anyone who is seriously studying Paleoindian technology. This database is part of the public domain of American archaeology and is available at no cost to anyone requesting it.

Clovis type – named by Edgar B. Howard in 1935 after a city in New Mexico. It is a small-to-large lanceolate point with a fluting that is usually small-to-medium in length. Base is concave and ground. Type dates 9500 to 9000 BC and is found all over the U.S.
Reference: Howard, Edgar B. (1935) Evidence of Early Man in North America. The Museum Journal, Vol. 24, pp. 2-3, University of Pennsylvania Museum.

According to Wormington (1957), the Clovis point is:
>   *Fluted lanceolate points with parallel or slightly convex sides and concave bases. They range in length from one and a half to five inches but are usually some three inches or more in length and fairly heavy. The flutes sometimes extend almost the full length of the point but usually they extend no more than half way from the base to the tip. Normally, one face will have a longer flute than the other. The fluting was generally produced by the removal of multiple flakes. In most instances the edges of the basal portion show evidence of smoothing by grinding. Certain fluted points found in the eastern United States resemble the Clovis type, but they have a constriction at the base which produces a fish-tailed effect. These have sometimes been called Ohio points or Cumberland points. Many of these tend to be somewhat narrower relative to their length than other fluted points.*

Johnson (1989) provides a generalized Clovis definition:
>   *... it is a relatively thin (width/thickness ratio), lanceolate, fluted point with a slightly to deeply concave base and lateral and basal edge grinding, dating to before Dalton points.*

PROVENANCE	
1 – Point find location	Every point has a provenance that reflects where the Native American parted with it. For the Survey, the following are used: 1 – In situ (site) 2 – Property owner (site or surface) 3 – River association (surface) 4 – County (surface) 5 – Virginia (surface).
2 – Site type	Reference to the type of site that a point was found in.
BASICS	

Basics – this table contains terms, procedures, processes, and methods used to record Paleoindian fluted points that were found in Virginia. Each point that is submitted to the Survey is recorded using numerous items in this table. Terminology, etc. is based on Hranicky and McCary (1995), Johnson (1989 and 1993),

Hranicky (2003), Callahan (1979), Whittaker (1994), Waldorf (1984), and Justice (1995). Most of these recording concepts are found on the Survey recording form.		
Lanceolate – one of five styles of American projectile points. It has parallel sides, excurvate or straight blade edges, and a concave or straight base. Its best known form is the Clovis type. And, according to Collins (1999): *...an adjective referring to the shape of chipped stone pieces that have convex edges tapering to a point at one or both ends.* **Lanceolate Blade** – reference to a large projectile point which may or may not be fluted. It can refer to a large knife or blade. **Lanceolate Point Style** – refers to a parallel-edged, slender, usually long point that does not have waisting, notching, or shouldering. **Flute** – term fluted may be attributed to H. C. Shetrone of the Ohio State Museum to the late 1930s (Roberts 1938). It is a basal channel or flake removal that shows single or multiple flake scars. It thinned a point base and facilitated hafting. It is a major attribute of the Paleoindian points.		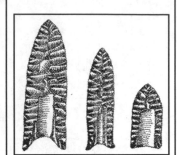
Point vs. Biface	The Survey's use of the term *point* as opposed to projectile point or biface has a long history. Regardless of contemporary archaeology's use and definitions, point will be used to refer to any Survey numbered point. Johnson (1989), who formerly ran the Survey, also prefers the term point as opposed to projectile point or hafted biface. However, the definition (typology) of a Clovis point is left to researchers.	
Projectile Point vs. Knife	Ageless argument in archaeology whether the Clovis point was used as a projectile point or as a knife. Toll morphology suggest the differences, but this is still controversial.	
Fluted vs. Unfluted	The Clovis lanceolate form occurs as fluted and unfluted specimens. Lack of the flute may indicate age within the Paleoindian period or lack of skill by the pointmaker.	
Course vs. Medium vs. Fine Grain Stones	Cryptocrystalline vs. crystalline. Particle size as a standard is suggested at ~2 to 100 nm in thickness and is based on clay.[27]	
Quarry vs. Local Stone Usage	Source: mining vs. pickup cobbles.	
Morphology	The study of shapes; typology. Term was not intended for the physical science (intended for living organisms); however, it is a study of structure and physical shape. It is the relationships among changes, modifications, or continued shape maintenance that may not always be observable for an archaeological analysis. In Clovis technology, it involves: 1 – Attribute positional notation(s), landmarks and benchmarks 2 – Design criteria within the social community 3 – Creation ability (and skill) by the knapper 4 – Variation of established (traditional) structure 5 – Work purpose (task type activity) or functional intentions 6 – Material composition and lithic durability 7 – Physical appearance or style 8 – Lithic curation practices 9 – Life cycle modifications (maintenance).	
ENTITY		
Form	A physical object representing time and culture. It contains recognizable traits and conformation attributes which allow it to be classified archaeologically.	
Persistent Attribute	A physical property that is consistent (always occurs) in an artifact or class.	
Persistent Trait	An artifact-specific property that usually varies by artifact but may	

---

[27] USGS has a program for calculation of particle size based on X-ray diffraction. Strain calculations are also possible.

	(or may not) occur on other members of a class or type
Uniqueness	All entities are unique; mo two artifacts are ever exactly alike.

<table>
<tr><td colspan="2" align="center">SURVEY PROCEDURES</td></tr>
<tr>
<td>

1 – Procedures, Processes, and Methods

This table contains the Survey's basic operations. It involves:

A – Receiving points for inclusion in the Survey

B – Recording the point

C – Making rubbings, drawings, and photographs (file/digital).

D – Submitting the point for Survey Committee review

E – Upon acceptance, adding the point's data to the Survey database

F – Publishing the point (with others) in the Quarterly Bulletin of the Archeological Society of Virginia.

</td>
<td>

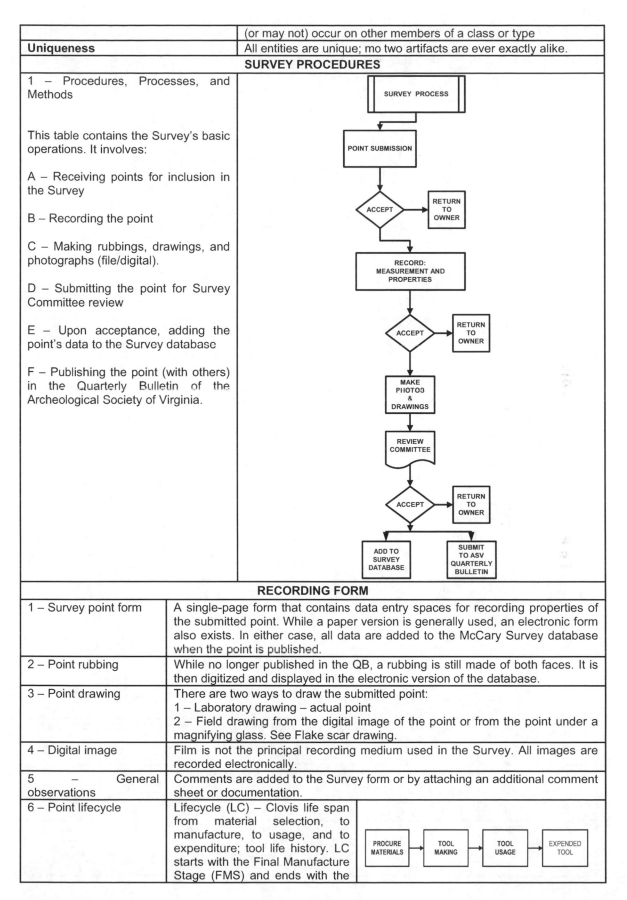

</td>
</tr>
</table>

	RECORDING FORM	
1 – Survey point form	A single-page form that contains data entry spaces for recording properties of the submitted point. While a paper version is generally used, an electronic form also exists. In either case, all data are added to the McCary Survey database when the point is published.	
2 – Point rubbing	While no longer published in the QB, a rubbing is still made of both faces. It is then digitized and displayed in the electronic version of the database.	
3 – Point drawing	There are two ways to draw the submitted point: 1 – Laboratory drawing – actual point 2 – Field drawing from the digital image of the point or from the point under a magnifying glass. See Flake scar drawing.	
4 – Digital image	Film is not the principal recording medium used in the Survey. All images are recorded electronically.	
5 – General observations	Comments are added to the Survey form or by attaching an additional comment sheet or documentation.	
6 – Point lifecycle	Lifecycle (LC) – Clovis life span from material selection, to manufacture, to usage, and to expenditure; tool life history. LC starts with the Final Manufacture Stage (FMS) and ends with the	

	Final Usage Stage (FUS) or expention. Point is generally evaluated as to what stage it is in a normal point lifecycle. Note: It can be measured in lifecycle units of: 1LC = 4 seasons (12 months) Note: LC includes retrofitting and repair and still be measured in units.
7 – Point recording methods	There are three basic types of point recordings used in the Survey. Laboratory recording is when the point owner turns the point over to the Survey for analysis. This is the preferred method. Field recording is performed when someone from the Survey visits the point owner's place of residence or office. The third method is third-hand recording by someone, an agent for the Survey, who records the point and provides a certified report which is used by the Survey to number a point. The Survey may act as a third-party recorder for other state Surveys.
8 – Point numbering	In the early days of the Survey, McCary would record the point, then write that number on the point. The Survey does not place any notations on a Survey point, and recommends that others follow the same practice. However, a museum must have system inventory notations to track its collections.

Photographic Imaging

1 – Digital image	All point faces and profile are recorded using a digital camera. Digital imaging requires special lighting set-ups and computer software to make color corrections.
2 – Film imaging	All points submitted for laboratory analysis are recorded by camera and film. Close-up photographs are also made.

3 – Infrared imaging	All laboratory recording includes infrared imaging using three different spectrum frequencies and different lighting angles.

GENERAL

1 – Point recordation	Actual recording of properties of the point, which are: 1 – Field recording 2 – Laboratory recording 3 – Third party recording.
2 – Attribute vs. Property	Attribute is a condition that is found in the Clovis type; whereas, property is a condition of the point that is being studied. Note: Trait is not used for a specific point; term refers to the Clovis type in general.

3 – Fluted vs. nonfluted	Generally, only fluted points are recorded in the Survey; however, some Clovis points were not fluted and; thus, they may be included. Also points, such as the Simpson and Suwannee were recorded by Ben McCary, and they will probably be included in future Survey reports. Cumberland points will be included, but none have been found in Virginia.
4 – Point submission	Application, by letter, email, or verbally, for a point to be considered for inclusion in the Survey. Application must include permission to publish, but the owner can remain anonymous.
5 – Completeness	Point is recorded as: 1 – Complete 2 – Broken.
6 – Morphology	Reference to the general shape of the point; its style excluding resharpening. Basic forms: • Lanceolate • Fishtailed • Triangular • Excurvate-bladed • Parallel-sided • Waisted/shouldered Shape is often equated to Early, Middle, and Late Paleoindian Periods (Gardner 1989). Shoop Site Examples, Pennsylvania
7 – Shape	Even with resharpening, point should have a symmetrical appearance. Shape is a reference to the physical topology of the point.
8 – Benchmark	Analytical reference which may be an estimate or count from which a measurement can be made. Measurement from a specific landmark to another landmark on a tool. As an analytical tool, it is a system of establishing tool class and/or industry frequencies within a river drainage, county, state, region, or nationally. Once a benchmark is established, any other site's material can be compared to it. The Survey greatly contributes to benchmarking Clovis technology in Virginia.
9 – Landmark	For all points, it is defined as specific attributes needed to define a tool in a class. Landmarks are assumed to be related to tool function and purpose. For points, it is a reference to major parts, especially attributes which are common to all points: 1 – Point tip 2 – Medial axis 3 – Blade edge 4 – Shoulder 5 – Notch, if present 6 – Stem, if present 7 – Base. Model for all Points
10 – Approximal fragment	Estimation of a broken point's original shape. Drawing represents McCary Survey Number 394.

11 – Point profiles	Sectional view of the midline of a point from its distal end to the point's base. It is the opposite of cross view. Length-wise profiles are drawings for Survey points that have laboratory analysis. See Florida example below.	
12 – Knapping signature	Style and knapping which is high-quality so as to identify the makers; special ways of knapping.	
13 – Supportive materials	Artifacts/debris that were found within close association with the record point are recorded separately and become part of the Survey paper records. This material also may include written records/photographs about/of the record point.	
14 – Walk-in point	Reference to an authentic point that was found outside Virginia and it suddenly comes to Virginia for inclusion in the Survey.	
15 – Record point	A fluted point that has a McCary Survey number.	
16 – Point removal	Generally, after a point has been in the Survey for several years, it is never removed. However, if at such time evidence shows it to be a fake, it will be removed. The point's number will not be re-issued for numbers below 1000.	
17 – Re-chipped point	Reference to re-chipping a broken point into a modern repro point. This practice usually fails the ultraviolet test. Note: Retrofitting a point does occur on Native-era points.	
18 – Ground	Deliberate smoothing of point edges used for hafting. Values are: light, moderate, and heavy. This is a subjective evaluation based on experience.	

DIMENSIONS		
1 – Metrics	All measurements are recorded in millimeters, grams, and centigrade degrees. All measurements are presented to significant digits.	

2 – Basic Measurements	The following measurements are used:
	1 – Maximum length 2 – Maximum width
	3 – Maximum thickness 4 – Concavity height
	5 – Concavity width 6 – Base width
	7 – Flute_Face_A1 width 8 – Flute_Face_A1 height
	7 – Flute_Face_B1 width 8 – Flute_Face_B1 height
	
	Each of these measurements (ordinality) is on the Survey record form and is maintained in the Survey database as primary data. These data are also used to calculate point ratios. See Georgia point drawing below.
	
	Each point measurement is recorded to one significant decimal digit, such as:
	    59.0 mm
	    7.9 mm	

3 – Measurement – length	Linear measurement of a point; length of longest axis, called ordinality. It refers to the distance from the proximal to distal end in millimeters.
	
	Note: Not presently used, but:
	
	The original length of a resharpened point can always be expressed as:
	
	    $\alpha = \log(1/L)$
	
	whereas:
	    1 = arbitrary whole entity
	    α = original, but unknown length
	    L = measured length.
	
	Point length estimation method is defined in Hranicky and McCary (1995). It is not used on the Survey record form, but can be calculated from the database.	

4 – Measurement – width	Maximum distance across the point's face.	

5 – Measurement – thickness	Maximum distance through the point's face.
6 – Basal concavity	Type of basal indentation. It includes grinding or flaking analyses.
7 – Concavity height	Measurement from the base to the top of the concavity.
8 – Concavity width	While somewhat difficult, it is a measurement of the widest part of the concavity.
9 – D/P profile	Refers to the flatness and thinness of a point's profile. It is calculated by dividing the proximal thickness mm by distal thickness mm; 1.00 represents a very flat profile. This number is called the Johnson ratio.[28]
10 – Base ratio	Base ratio is calculated as base length divided by base width. 1. Short (< 0.7) 2. Proportionate (> 0.7 to < 1.3) 3. Long (> 1.3).
11 – Blade ratio	Blade ratio is calculated as point length minus base length, and then divided by point width. 1. Lanceolate (> 2.0 mm) 2. Isosceles (< 2.0 to > 1.2 mm) 3. Equilateral (< 1.2 mm).
12 – Blade height	Measurement from the medial axis to the maximum point on the blade's curve.
13 – Blade curvature	Blade curvature is measured by drawing a lateral blade cord height measured from a line drawn from the tip of the point to the corner of the shoulder. 1. Very convex (> 5 mm) 2. Convex (< 5 mm to > 2 mm) 3. Straight (< 2 mm to > -2 mm) 4. Concave (<< -2 mm) 5. Mixed (< 2 mm to > 2 mm).
14 – Chassis (hafting) ratio	Chassis ratio is calculated as stem (top of grinding) length divided by base width. 1. Short (< 0.7) 2. Proportionate (> 0.7 to < 1.3) 3. Long (> 1.3).
15 – Blade ratio	Blade ratio is calculated as point length minus stem length, divided by point width. 1. Lanceolate (> 2.0 mm) 2. Isosceles (< 2.0 to > 1.2 mm) 3. Equilateral (< 1.2 mm).
16 – L*T/W ratio	Ratio is calculated by length times thickness divided by width; then divided by 100.
17 – Concavity measurement	Distal base concavity is measured as: 1. Convex (Positive base concavity less than or equal to -1 mm) 2. Straight (Concavity less than 1 mm and more than -1 mm) 3. Concave (Negative concavity greater than or equal to 1 mm).
18 – IEEE standards	Established procedures and methods in studying all aspects of stone artifacts. None are available for lithic technology (Hranicky 2002). When such becomes available, it should be written as a Standards Document and at a national level. Currently, professional archaeology implies but does not control standards. For metric standards in the U.S., the following are used for the Survey: ANSI/IEEE (std 260-1978) Standard Letter Symbols for Units of Measure ANSI/IEEE (std 268-1992) American Standards for Metric Practice.
19 – SI system & standard	System International (SI) is a convenient metric system of units that is used for all lithic technology investigations. They were developed by the International Bureau of Standards and have been used in the world since 1960. For the SI System, the International Organization for Standardization (ISO) has been successful in making SI the standard in scientific laboratories world-wide. The ISO was founded in October 14, 1946 in London and now is based in Geneva,

---

[28] Named by the author (Hranicky 2002) after Michael F. Johnson, who is the Fairfax County (Virginia) archaeologist. In addition to his archaeological abilities, he is a skilled flintknapper, especially working quartzite.

	Switzerland. It has 123 member nations, and the American National Standards Institute (ANSI) is the U.S. representative.
	The following are SI standards:

Quantity	Unit	Symbol
Length	meter	m
Mass	kilogram	kg
Time	second	s
Electric Current	ampere	A
Matter	mole	mol
Luminous intensity	candela	cd

The units are obtained from the product or quotient of base units:

Quantity	Expressed	Unit	Symbol
Volume	m^3		
Velocity	m/s		
Force	$kg * m/s^2$	newton	N
Work	$kg * m^2/s^2$	joule	J

20 – Specific gravity	Point's displacement property when submerged in water. SG is the ratio between the mass of the sample and the mass of an equal volume of a standard material, usually water. It is based on the concept that water at 4ºC (precisely 3.98ºC) is 0.999973 g/cm^3 or 1.000000 g/ml. Common Virginia rock ranges from 2.2 to 2.7 and the weight per cubic foot ranges from 150 to 190 pounds, depending on the nature of the constituent minerals and the porosity of the rock. Starting with MC 1000, a specific gravity (SG) measurement is made for points that are submitted for laboratory analysis. The readability is 0.001 gram. The formula used is: SG = (sample weight in air) / (sample weight in air) – (sample weight in water) Note: It is an excellent indicator of possible stone material. As a standard: **SG = 2.65**
21 – Point tip angle	Measurement of the type or style of the main body of a point tip. The major shapes are: 1 – Needle = >3 to 11 degrees 2 – Acuminate = >11 to 22 degrees 3 – Acute = >22 to 44 degrees 4 – Pointed Broad = 44 to 90 degrees.
22 – Flakes per centimeter (F/CM)	Measurement across the widest part of the point that counts the number of removed flakes and averages them to number per centimeter. Average can be a vertical count. Technique is often used in fluted point surveys and on high-quality flaked artifacts. The assumption is the more flakes per centimeter, the *better made* is the point. This count was started by Ben McCary and remains in practice. He used a Linen Tester glass which is still used by the Survey. Its validity as a qualitative measurement may be questionable.
23 – Color measurement	Based on the American Society for Testing and Materials (ASTM), Standard E 308-85, the color standards (recommended) are: • Blue (450 nanometers – λ) • Green (550 nanometers – λ) • Red (600 nanometers – λ) All colors are measured with these RGBs being the benchmark.
24 – Color change	Analysis to determine if a stone has been heat treated, See ΔHeat.
NOMENCLATURE	
1 – Blade modification	Any modification to symmetry that changes the leaf-shaped basic blade design.

	This modification often indicated a change in function (Hranicky 2002) of: 1 – Drill 2 – Scraper 3 – Burin (perforator) 4 – Spokeshave 5 – Others.
2 – Blade	Reference to the area that starts at the basal lateral grinding and extends to the tip of the point. It is referred to as the point's workend.
3 – Face 1	Prominent or best side of a point; display side; dorsal view.
4 – Face 2	Second face or reverse side of a point; labeling side; ventral view.
5 – Patination face	Side facing up during its occupation of the aging environment; however, it often can only be observed microscopically.
6 – Blade shape	Area above the ground lateral (shoulder) which ends at the point's tip. Basic blade edge shapes are: 1 – Straight 2 – Convex-excurvate 3 – Concave-incurvate 4 – Triangular 5 – Recurved 6 – Parallel-sided 7 – Irregular. Each blade edge may be: 1 – Mirror copy of each other 2 – Nonmirror copy of each other 3 – Curve shapes can be superimposed on either side.
7 – Bold	When used to describe lateral flaking or fluting, means that the flake scars are deep and in most cases also broad. Strong undulations are usually present.
8 – Beveled	Refers to an edge of a point that has been heavily flaked on one face. The effect is that the cutting edge is pushed off center toward the opposite face. Often with Palmer-Kirk points, both edges have been beveled, but in opposite directions; it probably does not apply to Clovis technology, but single face beveling does occur. This produces a slight but often noticeable twist to the blade when looking at the point from the tip.
9 – Serration	While common on later point types (Dalton, etc.), blade serration does occur. Tooth type, depth, width, and spacing are measured. Serration is any deliberate raggedness of a blade edge, usually in the form called tooth projections. Serration occurs on pre-Clovis blades.
10 – Burin	Is a kind of flake that removes an edge, producing a smooth, flat surface where the cutting edge was previously (see drawing below).
11 – Distal/proximal	Refers to the direction of the tip (distant). The opposite is proximal (close), which refers to the direction of the base.
12 – Finely/well made.	Is a qualitative term which means that the point is relatively thin, has an even surface with few bumps or major knapping errors, has a flat or lozenge shape cross section, and is systematically flaked, such as parallel flaking. Fine assumes use of outré passé flaking. The basic categories are: 1 – Fine 2 – Good 3 – Fair 4 – Poor.
13 – Outré passé (cross the medial axis) flake	While it refers to a type of flake scar, it is used to indicate consistency in the flake scars. It is a crucial consideration for accepting a point as being Clovis.
14 – Arris (center ridge)	Scientific term for ridge or crest. And, according to Collins (1999): *...the ridge or crest formed by the intersection of two flaked planes or facets, either on the face of a core or on the exterior of a flake or blade.*

15 – Medial axis (arris)	Center line of a tool that runs from the distal to proximal ends. It is used as a benchmark from which measurements are made. It is the vertical center by knapper's Final Manufacture Stage (FMS). Resharpening can alter the medial line but not the axis.	

16 – Hinge/step fracture	Is produced when a flake fails to carry to a smooth finish and breaks off leaving a step-like scar. Bumps and precipitous thick spots on a face are often the result of a hinge or step fracture. Flutes often end in such a way. Being able to correct or avoid such an error is a sign of a competent knapper. When a flake is removed, striking energy travels through it and terminates (is expended) at the end of what becomes the flake or flute. This end termination is recorded as: 1 – Absect – broken end 2 – Feather 3 – Step 4 – Hinge 5 – Round 6 – Overshot 7 – Axial 8 – Rising 9 – Irregular.
17 – Basal Corners	Basal corners on Clovis points are rarely sharp or points. The corner is usually rounded and ground.
18 – Water worn	Points found in or very near to rivers and lake will sometimes have worn surfaces due to water abrasive actions. This is true for points found on Virginia's continental shelf. Constant water is a factor in the point's patination.
19 – Flute numbering	All flutes are identified by their face designation, namely A and B. Face A's flutes are A1, A2, etc. Older flutes can be isolated, then A1.1 or below A1.1.1.

Profile of a Florida Point (Based on: Bullen 1975)

Burin on a Pennsylvania Clovis

Point Metrics as Used by the Georgia Survey

MATERIALS

1 – Lithic Material	Reference to the stone used and its knappability. Lithic source is added to the Survey record if known. Johnson and Pearsall (1998) set the lithic standard which was adopted from the Simplified Geological Map of Virginia (Bailey 1999) of the College of William and Mary.
2 – Patina	Judgment of the weathering effect on point's surface.
3 – A and B faces	Numerous points show differences in the degree of patination on each face. The heaviest patinated face is called the A face. Note: A and B faces are not necessarily the same as Face 1 and 2 used in point descriptions.
4 – Patinated	Reference to the degree of surface patination and recorded as: 1 – Heavily 2 – Moderately

	3 – Lightly 4 – None visible.	
5 – Weathering	Patination should not be uniform over the surface, and especially, it should differ from one face to another. Weathering is a process that is dependent on moisture (varies over time and space) and the point's buried chemical environment. Hranicky (2003) suggests a distributional condition map which may contribute in the future patination build-up studies. Note: Not currently used in the Survey; further testing is required.	
6 - Lithic Determinism	School of thought in archaeology that proposes the lithic preference by the Indians was such an important factor that it influenced their behavior, social organization, and migrational pattern. Paleoindians had a preference for certain fine-grain materials, namely flints and cherts.	Lithic access - availability of desired lithic materials to a social unit. It involves camping at a lithic outcrop, travel to and from a quarry site, or transportation of lithic materials over long distances. Lithic sourcing uses geological methods of tracing stone to its outcrops.
7 – Stone workability	Knappability or workability is based on Crabtree (1972) and Callahan (1979). Unless a special stone, scale is not generally noted in the point's survey record. All lithic material can be identified by using characteristic physical properties and molecular structure. Material may have a unique color, texture, or melting point. These properties do not depend on the quantity of the material and are called intensive property. Density also is an intensive property	
MANUFACTURE		
1 – Manufacture	Point should be thin and well-made (badly made points do occur in prehistory). In lithic technology (archaeology), it is procedures, methods, and skills needed to make stone tools from raw materials. It is tool construction from raw material to Final Manufacture Stage (FMS). Generally, manufacture refers to the cultural process based on knapping skills; whereas, production is a mechanical process, based on the Laws of Nature.	
2 – Stone carrier	Lithic material used to make the point. Every knappable stone has a workability factor (see Callahan 1979).	
3 – Flake scar	Area where a flake was removed; impressions of flake removal; negative images of flakes.	
4 – Flake scar drawing	Drawing showing the outer lines of flake scars. Technique produces a similar image as that of a point rubbing.	
5 – Remnant flake scar	It is a flake scar which has been overlaid by a later flake scar. It is rarely found on Clovis points.	
6 – Flaking identification	General and specific observations are made about flaking, which include: 1 – Interior – flake scars that do not extend to any biface edge 2 – Exterior – flake scars that originate (or terminate) on a biface edge 3 – Shaded – partially remaining flake scar that was flaked over by another flake removal 4 – Winged-edge – two flake scars, one on opposite face, sharing the same biface edge 5 – Diagonal – flake scars running across the face at an angle to the biface base	

	6 – Parallel – flake scars running across the face parallel to the biface base 7 – Random – irregularly-placed flake scars 8 – Shallow – scars that have a depth up to 3 mm 9 – Deep – scars that have a depth greater than 3 mm 10 – Error – any flake scar showing a nonnormal flake removal, such as a hinge flake 11 – Fan – flake scar starts at the edge and spreads outward toward the center 12 – Channel – narrow, long flake scar 13 – Irregular – usually V-shaped, but no distinct pattern 14 – Retouch – small edge scars caused by resharpening 15 – Island Flake – located in the middle of a biface. It has later scars on all sides 16 – Full medial – scar that starts at the edge and extends to the medial ridge or axis 17 – Post medial – scar that starts at the edge and extends past the medial ridge or axis.
7 – Irregular flaking	Means that the scars show that the knapper was opportunistically removing flakes. Flake scars look random, which they probably were not since they are of varying lengths, widths, depths, and show no definite pattern or sequence of removal.
8 – Selective flaking	Means essentially the same as irregular flaking, but may have minor patterning. It may be used to imply knapper avoidance for certain flake/scar configuration that would have damaged/destroyed the point.
9 – Systematic or patterned flaking	Refers to flake scars that indicate the removal of flakes in a sequence along an edge, such as the first flake being removed from the tip area and the last from the edge of the base. It involves scar size, depth, and spacing. Common references are parallel flaking or lateral retouching.
10 – Relatively systematic flaking	While other segments may not be. Usually, flakes removed in this manner leave scars that are similar in length, width, and depth, with later scars slightly overlapping the one immediately preceding them.
11 – Grinding	Refers to smoothing of the base and stem. It is classified as light, moderate, or heavy. Absence of grinding often means it is not a Clovis point. This is a basic characteristic (attribute) of this type. Grinding facilitated hafting.
12 – Polishing	Refers to smoothing on the blade's face.
13 – Alternate flaking	Refers to removing a flake from alternating faces.
14 – Waisting	Refers to a constricting or indented stem.
15 – Scarring	Refers to any impact or excessive force applied to the point that causes scarring or chipping. Generally, it refers to adverse or mistake flaking.
16 – Retouch	Blade edge that shows rejuvenation; short flake scars.
17 – Expention	Point blade is exhausted.
18 – Flute termination	Refers to the end (distal) of a flute scar. Channel usually feathers or hinges out.
19 – Flutes	Single or multiple flake scars, noting overlaps, but are numbered as: 1 - Flute 1 - first or prominent flute on a point; face or side called number 1. 2 - Flute 2 - second or next flute size on a point; face or side called number 2.
20 – Fluting	The flute channel is the area left on a point's surface when the flute flake was removed; flake groove. Flute channels should be smooth and rarely hinged out. The following techniques can be observed on Virginia Clovis points: 1 – Punch-off flute 2 – Antler struck (nipple set up) 3 – Pressure flute. There are three basic flutes (channels): 1 - Simple - single flute scar 2 - Multiple - two or more flute scars 3 - Composite - one flute scar on top of another scar. Example of a Fluting Study
21 – Scar geometry	Balance of flake removal scars that shape the point. It also includes flake overlaps and hinges.
22 – Flake scar orientation	Point was usually made by a structured (mental template) method and flake scars have a "Clovis orientation" that can be identified. This analysis can lead to knapping signatures.

23 – Blade edge	Outer edge (area) of a point is designed for cutting. There are six basic edge types used in the Survey: 1 - Curved 2 – Flat 3 - Trapezoidal 4 - Fractured 5 - Bibeveled 6 - Wedge. Note: Edge shape is not presently recorded.	CURVED FLAT TRAPEZOIDAL FRACTURED WEDGE BEVELED
24 – Basal thinning	Reference to small flakes removed from the base after fluting.	BLADE EDGE FLUTE BASAL FLAKING (THINNING)
25 – Blade reduction	Reference to type of blade reduction based on the basic Clovis morphology model. For Clovis normal usage, blade reduction (wear and resharpening) maintains the basic point style symmetry.	LINES OF EXPENDEDNESS POINT
26 – Lateral blade thinning	Flakes removed from either side by pressure (or percussion – rarely) flaking which causes thinning across a point's face. Thinning flakes rarely cross the medial axis. For Clovis, these flakes are usually parallel flaking.	
27 - Step fracture	In knapping, the energy travels through the stone and then suddenly turns upward producing a step fracture. In some cases, the energy turns downward. It is similar to a hinge fracture.	
28 - Hinge fracture	Break at the distal end of flake that was premature; hinge fractures break at right angles; break at the distal end of flake that was premature. And, according to Collins (1999): *...a detachment in which the force fails to carry to a thin, tapered termination, leaving a rounded distal edge (convex) on the flake and a rounded (concave), step-like scar on the parent piece; generally thought of as a knapping error.*	
29 – Lateral base-margins thinning	In conjunction with lateral blade thinning, the lateral margins of the stem area are usually thinned. Flaking is usually parallel pressure flaking.	

| 30 – Cross section (general for all points) | Mid-sectional view of a point; blade edge to edge view, as opposed to profile view which is a cross sectional view from distal end to base. The cross section of a projectile point reflects the histomorphology better than any single attribute.

Note: Counterfeit points often have incorrect cross sections. Clovis has:
1 – Lenticular
2 – Flat (blade)
3 – Fluted. | HEXGONAL RECTANGULAR DIAMOND RHOMBOID

OVATE PENTAGONAL TWIST DIAGONAL

OVAL TRAPEZODAL D-SHAPED TRIANGLE

PIE-SHAPED RIDGED FLUTED

CRESCENT WEDGE PRISMATIC
Cross Sections for all Types |

HAFTING

1 – Chassis	Area below the blade that was used to haft the point to a shaft or handle. Area is usually ground. The point and hafting apparatus are called the chassis assembly.
2 – Grinding height	Lower lateral grinding from base to shoulder (start of blade) is assumed here as a hafting area.
3 – Shoulder juncture	Shoulder juncture is a subjective evaluation of the form of the juncture between the stem (hafting area) and the base of the blade.
3 - Hafting coefficient	Base/stem/height angle is divided into the stem width/thickness product which produces a hafting coefficient for mathematically describing the mounting efficiency of points. Note: Coefficient was developed by Wm Jack Hranicky (1994) and has not been completely tested for use as a ratio.
4 - Hafting mass ratio	For points, this ratio indicates function, whereby: If, $$H^2/B < 1 = \text{penetration function}$$ Or if, $$H^2/B > 1 = \text{cutting function}$$ whereas: H^2 = hafting mass (see argument) B = blade mass. Argument: since there is no actual measurement which can be determined for a prehistoric haft, the square of hafting mass is assumed here as an approximate mass. Note: This is an untested hypothesis suggested here by Jack Hranicky.
5 - Hafting strength ratio	Ratio of point length to its haft length times its thickness, as: $$r = TL / HL * T$$ whereas:

94

	r = ratio TL = total length HL = haft length T = thickness.
6 - Haft/length ratio	Hafting ratio for length of point versus its hafting area: $$HL = a/b$$ whereas: HL = ratio a = length b = haft length.

PHYSICAL PROPERTIES		
1 – Impact fractures	Microscopic chipping caused by impact should be present on the tip. In some cases, major impact scars are present.	
2 – Breakage	Broken point types. Prehistoric breakage indicates function and use, which can be correlated to morphology and lithic material. Broken points can actually yield more data than complete points as they usually reflect the daily use of lithic tools by the Indians. Point breakage can be classified as (based on Curry, O'Brian, and Trimble 1985): A – Impact break – creates a broken tip or point of the blade. Break is perpendicular to the point of stress. Heavy stress due to impact may also cause a lower transversal break on the blade. B – Longitudinal break – occurs from the distal end to some position on the blade edge. Break parallels the center line. C – Diagonal break – starts high on one blade and ends lower on the other blade edge. An angular break is a break across the point. This type of break is usually caused by impact fractures where the impact energy did not travel through the blade in an even pattern; energy curved to one side of the blade edge. D – Reflaking break – occurs when reworking or resharpening a point. It is especially common when blades were percussion flaked. E – Transversal break – occurs across the blade from side to side. Break is at a right angle to the center line. F – Thermal break – caused by thermal action and occurs anywhere on the point. Potlid fractures are examples of this breakage. Color changes or surface glazing is also usually present. G – Crushing – practice may have occurred in using the point ceremonially; however, this practice is difficult to discern.	Basics for all projectile points:
3 – Stress breakage	Two major types are usually recorded for broken points: 1 – Snap – point breakage due to blade stress because of prying or twisting 2 – Impact – point breakage due to striking another object, such as bone,	

	wood, or stone.
	Stress (Breakage) – level at which stress overcomes lithic resistance and stone breaks.
	
	$$S = \zeta\,(b{>}r)t$$
	whereas:
	    s = stress
	    b = breakage level
	    r = max. resistance level
	    t = time.
	
	Stress is always a relationship of force and time, but is mainly a breakage function of the structure of the lithic material, for example basalt has a lower breakage level than chert.	

4 – Breakage (when)	Based on patination, breakage is classified as: 1 – During Paleoindian times 2 – Post-Paleoindian times.
5 – Broken point	Reference as used in the Survey: any point that has a fracture that separates the point into parts; not as originally manufactured by the Paleoindian.
6 – Breakage (classes)	Broken parts can be classified as: 1 – Proximal fragment 2 – Medial fragment 3 – Distal fragment 4 – Nondeterminant.

7 – Breakage (recording)	Notation from location-to-location on a blade or stem showing (B) cause (structural failure) or results (functional usage failure):
	
	$$B\,\zeta\,a,b$$
	
	whereas:
	    a = one location (start position)
	    b = one location (final position).
	
	Note: Being tested; not currently stored in database.

8 – Point symmetry	Concept was suggested by J. Hranicky (Hranicky and McCary 1995) which suggests resharpening maintained the original point outline. It may only apply to paleopoints.
9 – Ferric isolation	Method used for flint points (especially Clovis points) to determine their authenticity (Hranicky 2002 and 2003). It uses a principle that a substance in flint serves as an electron donor (oxidizer) and the substance which is the electron acceptor (reducer). This is an oxidation-reduction redox reaction that is present in the paleoenvironment and can be treated as: $$O_x + ne \leftrightarrow R_{ed}$$ For the Survey, it is the observation of ferric oxidation under hinges and along flake scar edges.
10 – Hemoglobin	End point in the process of selective precipitation for protein in a solution; also

crystallization (blood residue)	called protein fractionation. Crystallization is basically a process of dehydration of molecules in a solution. Each crystallized protein depends on the solution pH, ionic salts, and temperature. Technique involves growing hemoglobin crystals which are recognizable.
11 - Blood residue testing	Available and recommended for the point's owner. All residues have a common structural feature in lithic technology, as: $$O$$ $$\uparrow$$ $$NH_2 - CH - C - O - H$$ $$\downarrow$$ $$G$$ whereas: N = nitrogen H = hydrogen C = carbon O = oxygen G = an organic group. Test compound Benzedrine (4-4' diamino biphenye) has a sensitivity of 2×10^{-6} parts of blood (Hawk, Osen, and Summerson 1947).	Also, amino testing may be an analytical prospect. The primary difference among various amino acids is the nature of the side chain group, G, example shown here.
12 – Water test solution	For laboratory analysis, the point is placed in warm distilled water for 12 hours. The solution is tested for heavy metals and rare elements that might not occur where the point was found. A digital pH measurement is made. Note: NaCl is never tested because handling a point leaves a salt residue.
13 – Color (multicolor/single color)	Average color as best fits the point. The standard color reference is the Munsell chart. Both a visual color estimate and a Munsell number are maintained in the Survey database. Johnson and Pearsall (1998) set the color standard which was adopted from the Rock-Color Committee (in 1991) of the Geological Society of America. Note: Color is a subjective opinion, but can be measured electronically.
14 – Recording temperature	Degrees are taken primarily for adjusting color frequency observations. Note: It probably has little scientific significance.
15 – Heat treated	There is no significant evidence that heat treating stone was practiced among Clovis pointmakers, but specimens do occur. Heat treatment generally means a change in color or a shift in the stones infrared frequency (Hranicky 2004 and Collins and Fenwick 1974). Thermal alteration assesses indications of heat applied to the stone artifact. 1 - Altered refers to discoloration, crazing or potlids on the surface of the object. Discoloration, crazing and potlids indicate extreme heat. 2 - Unaltered is used when the surface of the object shows no evidence of intense heat. 3 - Indeterminate is used when the assessment of altered or unaltered cannot be made.
16 – ΔHeat	Delta heat, an estimate that a point's material was heat-treated for manufacture as opposed to thermal alteration caused by a later historic forest fire.
17 – Planar	Technique that represents a surface or face of a tool; surface area as on a tool face. It is an arbitrary assignment of space-measurement on a surface of an artifact. It is usually parallel lines across the longitudinal axis. Method allows microscopic examination of grid-assigned (numbered) areas. It is a similar approach to topographic mapping where a system of coordinates in a horizontal plane is used to describe the positions of points with

	respect to an arbitrary origin.	

USAGE AND WEAR PATTERNS		
1 – Wear/use patterns	Microscopic examination to determine blade edge usage. It involves identifying striations and polishes. Wear patterns are not tested on most survey points; for method, see Hranicky (2004) and Hoard, et al. (2004). User ware is damage on points that indicates contact with another substance. Wear pattern is damage on stone edges which results from the stone's contact with another substance.	
2 – Striation analysis	Microscopic lines that show patterns under a microscope; usually microscopic directional lines. Basic types are: 1 - Transverse striae 2 - Oblique striae 3 - Parallel striae 4 - Perpendicular striae 5 - Random striae 6 - Crossed striae. Point may be tested for usage patterns.	 Note: Test examples (Hranicky 2003).

MESAUREMENTS

Measurements (Rules) - numerous measurements are made about artifacts in archaeology. The following are recommended as standards:

□ All radiocarbon dates are rounded to the nearest 10 years, listed as BP, and always contain the year standard deviation, for example

5980 BP +/- 120 years

The last significant digit in the date and deviation is always zero.

□ All artifact dates older than 10,000 BC should be converted as:

12,000 BP.

□ All measurements are presented in millimeters and, if a decimal place is used, a .5 is used, for example:

33.0 mm
33.5 mm
34.0 mm

Note: Projectile point measurements are usually an exception with no decimal place.

□ All temperature measurements are given in degrees Celsius and contain no decimal, for example:

21° C
24° C

□ All statistical calculations are presented with three decimal places, for example:

Chi square 41.076

□ All ratios, indices, and percentages are presented with one decimal place, for example:

41.3%
1:1.4
 	
□ All counts of artifacts are presented without a decimal, for example:
 	
    512 flakes
    34 sherds
    91 points
 	
□ Any definition or conversion is presented without a decimal, for example:
 	
    1 kg = 1000 g
 	
□ All calculations are presented with the figure that contains the least number of significant figures, for example:
 	
    Sherd A sample average = 127.134 as 127.1
 	
    Sherd B sample average = 41.2 as 41.2
 	
    Sherd C sample average = 66.16 as 66.2
 	
□ All angles are measured without a decimal place, for example:
 	
    50°
    90°	

Measurements (Points) Standards	Measuring point attributes is used to describe a point's dimensions which quantify its basic design. The dimensions (baseline) are used to compare points within and between types. The following is a primary attribute list for measurements (Luchterhand 1970): 1 - Axial length - maximum length of the point along its center axis. In cases where the base is concave, the measurement includes the basal radius or point corners. 2 - Blade length - length of the blade portion along the center axis of the point. In instances where the haft element is notched, this measurement extends as far as a line connecting the area where the notch sides intersect the edge of the blade. For C-shaped indentations, the top of the C is used for the base of the blade. 3 - Tang length - length of the tang portion of the point, including the basal radius in cases where the base is concave; otherwise, use point corners. 4 - Shoulder width - width of the blade portion of the point where the blade joins the tang or hafting element. 5 - Point width - maximum distance across the widest part of the point, which should be the shoulder or blade. 6 - Tang width - minimum width of the haft portion of the point. It is usually measured between the interior extremities of the notches, base of the blade for a stemmed point, and across the blade/haft junction for a lanceolate point. 7 - Base width - maximum width of the haft element of the point or distance between point basal corners. 8 - Thickness - maximum thickness of the point, usually along the medial ridge. 9 - Right/left notch depth - perpendicular distance from a line tangent to the point at both its base and its shoulder to a line parallel to it and tangent to the interior extremity of the notch.

	10 - Right/left notch width - distance between two points at which a line is tangent to the base and blade. 11 - Right distal haft inclination - for a notched point, the angle which the distal side of the notch makes with the central axis of the piece. For lanceolate points, the angle formed by the line tangent to the distal part of the hafting element with the central axis of the point. For a stemmed point, the angle formed by the shoulder to the stem with the central axis of the point. 12 - Right/left proximal haft inclination - for a notched point, the angle formed by the proximal edge of the notch with the central axis of the point. For a lanceolate point, angle formed by a line tangent to the proximal end of the piece with the central axis of the point. 13 - Basal radius - depth of the concavity or protrusion of, respectively, a concave or convex base measured parallel to the central axis of the point. 14 - Axial direction – moving from the proximal to distal end of the point, it is the maximum distance and constitutes the wedge angle of the point. It follows the medial ridge, but is not restricted to it. It is the path that energy contained in the point would follow into a target.

MISCELLANEOUS

1 – Apex angles (Hranicky 2003)	Reference to angles formed by using a point's tip as a starting place. The following are the basic lines to create point angles:
	
	A line – top line from base to point tip
	B line – bottom line from base to point tip
	C line – center line (medial axis)
	D line – top blade height line to point tip
	E line – bottom blade height line to point tip
	F line – top blade height line to blade edge
	G line – bottom blade height line to blade edge.
		Primary angles are:
		
		    H and I (blade angle)
		    A and B (apex angle).
		
		Correlation between the two angles can be argued for knife versus projectiling functions. See drawings below.

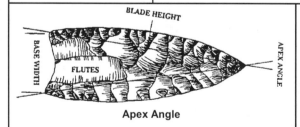 **Apex Angle**		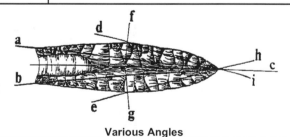 **Various Angles**
2 – Chassis assembly and ratio	Reference to the area, usually ground, for hafting which is: Ratio = Haft/Blade *100 This ratio is calculated in the database.	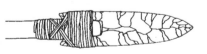
3 – Flute channel ripples	Compression Rings – ripple lines of force that radiate outward from the point of a blow that strikes a flake off stone. Undulation is another term for compression rings. It generally refers to rings on a blade when the force inward and downward	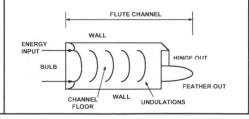

	was not equal.
4 – Flake scar ripples	Reference to the evaluation, quality, and methods in flake removal.
5 – Clovimetry plot – TWL	As part of the Clovisonian formulae, the TWL plot consists of three areas (T = max thickness, W = max width, and L = max length). The plot presents a three dimensional view of the relationships among a point's basic measurements (Hranicky 2003). Note: TWL plot is not applied to an expended point.
6 – Flake scar index	Mathematical relationship among flake scars indicating degrees (of flaking pressure) or configuration (arrangement of scars) which gives a measure of knappability on the part of the toolmaker. See Topographic Calliper below. Note: Currently not used (see Hranicky 2002).

7 – Length / thickness x width ratio	Point measurement by dividing the length by the width and multiplying this number by the width. Ratio is expressed as:
	
	$$L / T * W$$
	
	whereas:
	    L = length
	    T = thickness
	    W = width.
	Note: Not presently used, but can be calculated from the database.

8 – Length-weight product	Weight of the point in grams is multiplied by the length of the point in centimeters. Points that have a product of: 500 or less are arrow points, 500 to 1000 are spear points, 1000 and over are probably knives, ceremonial blades, or unknown. Note: Not presently used, but can be calculated from the database.

9 – Blade width/thickness ratio	Ratio for the point that can be translated into the point's strength. Ratio is determined by multiplying the point's thickness in centimeters by the point's width in centimeters. Point with a ratio of 10 or over can be considered as a thick/strong point – probably not Paleoindian. Basic ratio is:
	
	$$Ratio = B / T$$
	
	whereas:
	    B = blade width
	    T = thickness.
	
	Ratio is a point test which is based on a calculation in the database.

10 – Flute ratio	Maximum length of a point's flute divided by the length of the point.
11 – Length/width percentage	Knapping evaluation standard of determining the quality of the point's manufacture. The thinner the tool, the better the workmanship. Width is divided by length which is multiplied by 100. Note: Not presently used, but can be calculated from the database.

12 – Volume test	Approximate volume of a point can be measured by multiplying:
	
	$$V = L W T$$
	
	whereas:
	    V = volume
	    L = length
	    W = width
	    T = thickness.
	Note: Not used but can be calculated from the database.

13 – Point flake mapping	Process of breaking down the manufacturing stages of point manufacture. For example, flake scars are recorded by edge and then interior surfaces. Finally, flake sequencing is determined and drawn (Johnson 1993). Note: Method is not currently used in producing a point drawing for the Survey.	
ELECTRONICS		
1 – Ultraviolet (UV) test	Used primarily for testing a point for restoration and rechipping. Additionally, it is used to produce another visual view of the point. UV shows details that might not be observable under normal lighting conditions.	
2 – Topographic calliper	In testing. Will be used to map point topography digitally. In theory: Surface areas can be mapped as ^{+}S (high) or ^{-}S (low) which is based on index-marking area. In other words, areas are above (or equal to) or below the index area. We assume a boundary condition for each S, but in practice, this is a judgmental factor. ^{+}S areas are the first choices for flake removal. It can also be used at the surface's molecular level.	Flake Scar Index
3 – Digital calliper	Used for all point measurements. Standard tool for measuring points.	
4 – Patination analysis	Classified. Used by the Survey for laboratory authentication of points.	
DATABASE		
1 – Software	Survey uses Word, FrontPage, and Access 2000 for its recordkeeping.	
2 – Database backup	Database is backed up after any changes are made.	
3 – Data entry	Survey data are entered using a record entry program that was developed in Access.	
4 – Data structure	Database structure is defined in the McCary Survey Database document.	
5 – Data updates	Original Survey data are not changed. Updates are accomplished by re-recording a Survey point. A re-recording will be indicated by adding a decimal point and a number to the original Survey number. For example, MC 12 is noted as MC 12 (by McCary) in the database. Years later, it was re-re-recorded; it is noted in the database as a new record MC 12.1 (by Johnson and Pearsall), then a record MC 12.2 (by Hranicky), and so forth for any new re-recordings. Re-recording will generally increase the amount of data from a point. The database will contain the name (or institution) of the person making the new evaluation. In doing so, a researcher, can use the various point records for still new interpretations. Search functions can include or exclude re-recordings.	
3 – Server/PC	The Survey currently resides on a Dell PC with a redundant system on a Dell laptop.	
4 – Maintenance	Normal PC maintenance. Hard drives are changed annually.	
5 – Website – portal	To be architecture, www.mccary_survey.org	
6 – Database query	To be architecture, what-if scenarios.	
7 – Data mining	Procedure(s) to drill down in a database for specific combinations of data.	
MASS SPECTROSCOPY		
N_2 analysis	McCary Survey classified; available upon request.	
VISUAL PRESENTATION		
1 – Visual information	First-hand observations; physical properties that can be seen with the human eye.	
2 – 3-D images	To be architecture; multidimensional projections.	
3 – Discriminate Analysis (DA)	New Survey database which has point data from a predefined assemblage – type, and simultaneously measuring the value of each of the attribute variables against total point benchmarks; in making this distinction (as in Reyneir 1994), as:	

Attribute	Details of measurement and unit
Length	Maximum and estimated length mm
Width	Measured at widest point mm
Thickness	Measured at thickest point mm
Retouch length	Maximum length in a straight line mm
Estimated length	Statistical length at manufacture
Retouch depth	Measured at the mid-point mm
Retouch type	Abrupt, semi-abrupt, obtuse coded
Retouch class	Regular, micro, chaville, impacted, flaking coded
Lateralization	Left, right coded
Scar pattern	The number and position of the crest is coded
Angle of point	Measured at the tip to the nearest 5 degrees
Added retouch	Additional to the main retouched margin coded
Base type	Narrow, broad and estimated coded
Flute margins	Width, length, index, layers, etc.

More to be added as testing and evaluation continues …

FUTURE ANALYSES

1 – Production volume	The amount of stone needed to produce a single point. Michael Johnson has data of this type of study; also, see Hall and Larson (2004). Note: Needs Survey testing but see Hranicky (2004) for the concept.	
2 – Clovis life prediction	Tool life is predictable, but it is a cautious prediction. If we can assume a normal usage on expected targets (and temperature @ 75º), then tool (T), velocity (V), time (t), and life (L) should be: $$L \; \zeta \; Vt$$ Note: Concept has not been tested. Since most prehistoric tools (axes, knives, points, celts, etc.) are expended tools when found, predictive methods must backtrack to the tool's Final Manufacturing Stage (FMS). Also, this model does not account for lithic material. Additionally, tool life is affected by change in temperature and the magnitude of usage. All of which does complicate a prediction model.	

Appendix B – Survey Procedures

Notebook
Onion skin paper
  for rubbing
Digital calipers
Charcoal for
rubbing
Weighing scale
Magnifying lens
Munsell color scale
Digital camera
  for photographs
Topographic map
  for known
  provenance
Digital
Thermometer
	Apparatus, equipment, and supplies vary among archaeologists, but everything suggested here is basic to recording Clovis points.

		In order to perform the point analysis and recordation, certain material and equipment are needed. As these items must be portable, as most point owners do not want to let their point be taken to a laboratory. While laboratory conditions certainly are preferred, the recorder must make every effort to obtain all possible data about the point in a field survey.

Activity/Analysis	Procedure	Process
Manufacture	A Clovis is made using bifacial reduction techniques. Examine the point to determine what areas on the point show this process, namely percussion and pressure flaking scars. Next, determine and classify the point's basic shape (style).	Note: Blade-made points do occur.
Lithic Material	Determine the type of stone that the point was made from. If the material's source can be determined, note it in the point's record. Best examples are Thunderbird's jasper and Williamson's chalcedony. Stone analysis usually requires geology expertise. Use geology stone and gem books as a guide for identifying the lithic material.	May require analysis by a geologist. A second opinion is recommended.
Stone Workability	After identifying the stone, determined it workability. Use Callahan's (1979) scale.	Workability is a factor in stone selection, but more importantly, it is a factor in durability, cutting capability, and numerous other factors.
Dimensions	The first measurement is length. A measurement is taken from the proximal to distal ends of the point. Next, width is measured on the widest part of the point. Finally, thickness is measured from one face (through) to the reverse face. Calculate: 1 – Point length / width * thickness 2 – Blade width / thickness * length 3 – Blade / thickness 4 – Haft (grinding) / base width.	Basic matrix data are used for classification and evaluation. When data are combined with other point data, point distributions, chronologies, physical structures, and point functions can be established for specific geographical areas and the total Clovis populations.

		 MC 852
Benchmark Comparison	Evaluate the point against Survey (other) benchmarks. Justify the point's variability.	Tables that are available for data mining to determine metric correlations.
Length Estimation	Using the statistical length estimate presented earlier or in Hranicky and McCary (1995), calculate the point's statistical length. This value is based on Virginia's Clovis population and may not be valid in other areas.	Length is a function of usage; when the knapper attempted long points, the majority of found points show the results of blade reduction via usage.
L/W*T Ratio	Once the basic measurements have been taken, calculate the L/W*T ratio.	Ratio is an excellent indicator of the point's form and is used for analytical and comparative purposes.
Point Apex Angle	Using each basal corner, draw lines to the tip of the point. These lines are used to measure blade height and angle.	Indicates blade reduction; not used as a single measurement.
Tip Angle	 Using a small straight-edged board, place it at the widest point on the blade and let the other end cross the point's tip. Draw a line along the board; repeat the process without moving the point for the other side. Using a protractor, measure the angle of the crossing lines. Note: The blade height indicates the starting spot for the angle measurement.	Method measures the point tip angle which is used to determine a possible point function. Note: Angle estimates are obvious from the point's blade shape, but actual measurements can be used in statistical estimates of function or usage.
Concavity	Using a small straight-edged board, place it across the base of the point. Then use pointers or a caliper to measure the height of the concavity.	Method measures the height of the concavity which is assumed to be part of the hafting (chassis) assembly. The diameter can be used in estimating the point's chassis assembly.

	 Width of the concavity can be made; however, it is difficult to determine where each side starts. If performed, then calculate the diameter of the circle formed by extending its curve.	
Flute Measurements	Flutes are measured individually from the top of the concavity to the end of the flute scar. Flutes are labeled by point face and by number if multiple flutes occur. Number flutes (left-to-right) and by face. Calculate the flute ratio.	 Measurements determine the point's chassis assembly dimensions.
Blade Edges	Edges are recorded by style and retouch, if present. An estimate of the number of flakes per cm can be taken. 	The blade edge is the primary factor in determined usage. The edge usually has wear patterns which amply point function (s).
Blade Modification	While obvious, examine the point for blade modification, especially recurving and modification into biface bits. Also, broken blades were sometimes retrofitted.	Blade alteration is an indication of a change in the point's function.
Blade Heights	Calculate maximum blade height for each edge.	A factor in blade cutting capabilities.
Flake Scar Analysis	Flaking scar pattern should follow a Paleoindian way of making the point. This analysis is a continuation of the manufacturing technique. Make notes about flake scars, especially hinged flakes, step flaking, overstrikes, deep scar failures, island flakes, etc.	If flake scars are analyzed, recorded, and mapped correctly, knapping signatures can be identified.
Grinding Polishing	Basal grinding is a subjective evaluation based on experience. The finger is rubbed across the base and lower margins. A rough or sharpness indicates no basal grinding. Once this area starts becoming smooth to the feel, grinding is present. The range is from light to high smoothing. The human "lip" is sometimes used to test smoothing. The range is subjective, but at least, most tests show the presence or absence of basal grinding.	Grinding is a major trait in Clovis technology. It is assumed here to be a contribution to the point's chassis assembly.

By examining the ground area with high magnification, striations can be observed. As a suggestion, the grinding should go across the margin, not lateral to the margin. This is generally true on eastern points; however, it needs scientific testing.

Thinning	Thinning is an observation to determine if the point's lateral margins were systematically thinned. If the point shows small, but relatively long flake scars along the margins, it has been thinned. This condition is sometimes called retouch. Basal thinning is generally shows removal of very small flakes. After which, the area is ground.	Thinning serves to lighten the point and increase the cutting angle of the blade (frank).
Reworking	Any modification to the point's blade or stem area that indicates retrofitting. Reworking should show the point's change from its original shape or form. Term is sometimes used for resharpening.	Basic evidence of point maintenance, longevity, and probably usage (wear patterns).
Stem Reduction	Examine the area below the blade (chassis) to determine if the stem has been reduced to accommodate narrowing of the blade.	If present, this reduction shows retrofitting of the point; new hafting to replace a worn out assembly.
Point Style	Determine the basic style (shape) that was intended by the manufacturer. Expended points often do not reflect the point's original style. The following points are examples of point style variations. This is a continuation of the manufacturing process.	Style is probably a good indicator of geography and chronology, but since most points do not come from a site context, style remains speculative in archaeology.

MC 269	MC 420	MC 442	MC444	MC410

Weight	Use a digital scale and measure the point's weight in grams.	Weight is a volumetric indicator and can be used to determine flyability, chassis longevity, stone source, and numerous factors in the analysis of points.
Patination Analysis	Because of patination hiding the surface point's material, identification of lithic materials can be difficult. Determine the level of patination and note differences between faces, if any.	Lithic material is an excellent identifier of a point's life cycle distribution. Patination depth can be measured which may be assigned to local chronology.
Photographs	Make both digital and film images of the point. A light table and stand is needed. Ideally, the point is photographed using black and white film, negative film, and slide film. Photographs and images should show contrast to emphasized flake scars. Consult photography textbooks for this recording step. Note: There is a major difference in lighting for film versus digital photography.	Basic recording process.
Rubbing	Rubbings are made of both faces. By using white onion-skin paper, press the paper down on the point so as to cause the paper's surface to conform to the flake scars. Next, use a charcoal pencil, soft-lead pencil, or carbon block to lightly rub the surface. Record both faces.	Classic form of recording Clovis points.
Drawing	Drawings are a time proven technique for recording artifacts. Drawings can highlight special attributes. Drawings are made of both faces. Next,	Drawings provide abstract details that reinforce other recording methods. They are a time-tested

	drawings are made of the flute channels. There are three basic techniques: 1 – Make drawing by visually inspecting the point – hand drawn. 2 – Do rubbings, then overlay tracing paper and made the drawing. 3 – Create a digital image and print out an oversized image; then overlay tracing paper and ink-in flake scars. Note: An enlarged drawing of flutes and of the point's profile is common.	method. Numerous drawing styles and methods exist; used what is best for the recorder. Profile and cross section are shown in the next drawing.
MC 915	901	
Cross Section Drawing	Cross section is measured by examining (viewing) the point from the proximal end towards the distal end. Most points are bi-convex or plano-convex (D-shaped). Make a drawing of: 1 – Middle point cross section 2 – Proximal end cross section. Indicate point's thickness (mm) at the place that the drawing shows.	Cross section is a major attribute. T1 T2
Point Symmetry	The drawing is a good place to note irregular blade shapes, or areas on the blade where the user modified the point into another tool. Basically, blade sides should be mirror images of each other.	Symmetry has minor latitudes based on resharpening.
Flake Scar Mapping	Make a drawing of the flake scars noting their position and layering. For an example of this technique, see Johnson (1993).	Used to classify the point as Paleoindian.
Silhouette	Hranicky and McCord (1976) were the first to use silhouettes for identifying Virginia point types. The point's perimeter is outlined and then inked in.	It is used for quick identifications and typing forms (shapes).
Numbering a Point	Not recommended.	May harm the surface for future analyses.
Manufacture	Most Clovis points were made using the bifacial reduction technique. Percussion flake was used to shape the basic form; after which, pressure flaking was used to finalize the point. Record flake scars that indicate these methods.	Major attributes of the point.

	Note 1: Refer to the workability of the stone. Note 2: Some Clovis points were made from large core blades; they generally have a flatish cross section.	
Life Cycle	Determine the point's life cycle time/used condition. Statistics are a good tool for this appraisal.	The function of length determines a point's position in the normal Paleoindian tool life cycles; however, usage, material, and lithic availability are cultural conditions which need to be incorporated in the life cycle.
Point Grade	The recorder makes a subjective evaluation whether the point is a fine, good, fair, or poor point.	Probably too subjective to be useful.
Color Analysis	Color is determined by visually selecting a color from the Munsell color book. If several colors appear, make several notations. Make reading for both faces. Since temperature affects color, take a reading of the recording environment temperature. Note: The Munsell color scale is partially a subject observation, but none-the-less, a scientific observation. 	Color is a factor in material selection. In numerous cases, colorful stones were used by the Paleoindians. Color for multicolored stones is left to the researcher, but usually is classified as color x and color y.
Color Spectrum	Measuring a point's surface and determining a specific color frequency for that face.	Spectroradiomters, such as Hewlett Packard's HP 8452A can be used for color measurements.
Johnson Index	The Johnson Index is a Distal/Proximal ratio which is calculated from thickness measurements made 5 mm from each end of a point. Pointers are used to approximate the location for the measurement. No markings are made on the point, as this would be a destructive process for the point's surface – it must be as close of an approximation as possible.	It is a measurement of the flatness of a Clovis point, or a distal/proximal (D/P) ratio. A 3-digit caliper is used to provide a significant index number of three decimal places. This ratio converts the point's physical dimensions into a number, which is: Ratio <1, such as 0.999 (point generally tapers towards the tip) Ratio >1, such as 1.034 (point has above average basal thinning).

Planar Method	The planar method involves taking plus (+) or minus (-) measurements along the point's medial axis. Each face is measured. Measurements are taken at spaced intervals, a zero (0) line is created, and measurements are recorded when there is a (+) or (–) change. 	 Surface topography varies from point-to-point, but topography as a lanceolate trait (form) is universal.
Breakage	For broken points, determine if the break was Indian or post-Indian. Next, determine the type of break and assess possible causes for the break. 	Breakage determination is used to indicate tool usage and function.
Resharpening	Examine the point's edges for removal of small flakes. It often altered the initial shape of the blade. Resharpening will cause the edge to become thicker and it will often have thinning flakes.	This maintenance process indicates rejuvenation of the cutting edge. Resharpening will destroy life cycle stage (evidence) of usage.
Edgewear - Edge Striations	Note any deliberate edge working that creates a saw-like edge. However, these edges may have been caused by natural forces during the point's buried period. Use magnifying apparatus as: Low power (10-75x): Observe usewear scars, edge rounding or smoothing caused by contact with another substance. Can be divided into classes, such as: hard (bone, antler), medium (wood, hide), or soft (meat, plant).	Common trait is usewear.

	High power 80-500x or SEM): Can be used to determine the exact material that the edge was used on; even may show residue. See Microscopic examination below.	
Blood Residue	This testing is performed by a laboratory with test equipment and personnel needed to determine blood reside. If the point is a surface find, test will usually not produce valid results. For an example, see Loy and Dixon (1998).	Major indicator of point usage.
Chemical Testing	Survey uses water samples to make chemical test on the point's patination. See Survey staff for guidance. 	Used to determine Clovis fakes; especially the N_2 test.
UV Test	In a dark laboratory (room), take a UV light generator and pass it over the point's surface. Note any irregularities. Repeat for the reverse face. Note: Fluting channels are often re-formed on fakes. 	Fake or re-chipped points can sometimes be identified using this method.
Specific Gravity (SG)	First weigh the specimen in dry air. Then weigh the specimen submerged in water. Temperature at the time of analysis should be recorded. Make SG calculation. During this test, the point's volume can be determined.	Basic method in geology for determining stone types. Use quartz (SG 2.65) to calibrate equipment.

Microscopic Examination	Microscopic examination is the key process for determining a point's lithic history. Check the following: ☐ Impact fractures on the distal end. ☐ Blade edge chipping (retouch) ☐ Flake scar edges should not be sharp, wear or polish should be present ☐ Oxidation under the flake scars ☐ Weathering (Patination) should show differences, especially between faces ☐ Grinding should have consistent striations, but this is a difficult assessment. Contrast grinding with excavated points. ☐ Lateral flakes should show resharpening ☐ Flute channel walls should not be sharp and show wear striations ☐ Blade edges should show wear or polish; however, this may be absent due to resharpening	 Flute channel magnification on North Carolina Survey point NC-284. It shows ripples in its surface.
Making Cast	To make a cast, mix clay-like chemicals for creating a mold. Press the point into the mold and remove it. Next, poor the epoxy into the mold and let it set. Avoid attempting to replicate the point's color(s). Repeat the process to make as many copies as needed. Leave the edge overflow, as the basic point design has been captured. If two-sided casts are needed, submit the point to a professional casting laboratory	 Survey Casts of MC 26

Appendix C – Survey Policies

1 – Recordation	Record all authentic points and publish the records that are submitted to the survey.
2 – Point validation	Ensure that a point record represents a valid point. Maintain records of false and eBay points. Note: Fewer that 5% of the points for sale on eBay are authentic points. Keep records; these points will come to haunt surveys.
3 – Public realm	There is no such thing as private archaeology (McGimsey 1972). All point records belong to the public realm and should be available to anyone for study.
4 – Site location	Simply refer need-to-know requestors to state and federal agencies. Otherwise, report any site discovered during point recording.
5 – Point ownership	Reference to owner can be anonymous. Subsequent ownership is not tracked unless new owners provide this information to the Survey.
6 – Point receipt	When the Survey receives a point, a color-photo receipt is sent to the owner. Generally, it states that the point is under review.
7 - Database	The survey's database is public property and free to anyone who uses it in a scientific manner.
8 – Dollar value	The survey recognizes that points have monetary values, but makes no effort to establish or estimate dollar value.
9 – Scientific testing	Within limits of the owner, performs all scientific tests that are available to the survey.
10 – Requesting point submissions	The survey should advertise its services and objectives in **only** scientific journals and magazines.
11 – Educating the public	The survey will present lectures and provide displays that will educated the public about archaeology and the Paleoindian era.
12 – Indian concerns	The survey will remain sensitive to Indian concerns and report to local tribes any point that is found on federal property.
13 – Scientific principles	The survey will only used established scientific principles and methods as practiced by all scientific disciplines in general, and specifically in archaeology.
14 – Ethics	The survey will conform the ethical standards as set forth by the Society for American Archaeology.
15 – Survey ownership	The survey will not acquire artifacts.
16 – Review process	The survey will provide a review process for submitted points by establishing a review committee of professional and amateur archaeology and collectors.
17 – Dead point file	The survey will maintain a dead point file for rejected points which will include reasons why the point was not accepted in the survey.
18 – Written standards, polices, procedures, and practices	The survey will maintain written standards, polices, procedures, and practices for its operation.
19 – Stewardship	The survey will encourage state-wide monitoring of Paleoindian resources.
20 – State/Federal standards	The survey will conform to all published state/federal guidelines and standards – or note exceptions.
21 – Fraudulent points and practices	The survey will report any fraudulent activities to proper authorities.
22 – Site looting	The survey will report any site looting activities to proper authorities.
23 – Stolen points	The survey will publish stolen points – only if appropriate documentation is provided.
24 – Point distribution	The survey will maintain point distribution maps for its area of coverage, as in Hranicky and McCary (1995) and Brennan (1982).
25 – Point curation	The survey will provide advice for point curations and repositories.

114

Appendix D – Database Design

The following table provides the basic construct for a survey database. If the database principles discussed previously are used, then three (or more) relational tables should be used.

Point Database (Complex)				
Name	**Type**	**Size**	**Contents**	**Units/Value**
SPECIMEN	Number (Long)	4	Specimen Number	
ARTIFACT	VARCHAR	10	Artifact Number	
ARTIFACT_TYPE	Number (Integer)	2	Lithic Type	0 = Not Recorded, 1 = Uniface, 2 = Biface, 3 = Projectile Point, 4 = Drill, 5 = Utilized Flake, 6 = Scraper, 7 = Spokeshave, 8 = Knife
LITHIC_SHAPE	Number (Integer)	2	Lithic Shape	0 = Indeterminate, 1 = Lanceolate, 2 = Triangular, 3 = Pentagonal, 4 = Ovate, 5 = Discoidal, 6 = Square, 7 = Rectangle
STEM_CHARACTERISTICS	Number (Integer)	2	Stem Characteristics	0 = Indeterminate, 2 = Tapering, 3 = Parallel Sided, 4 = Expanding, 5 = Wide, 6 = Bifurcate, 7 = Side Notched, 8 = Corner Notched, 9 = Not Applicable
BASE_SHAPE	Number (Integer)	2	Base Shape	0 = Indeterminate, 1 = Pointed, 2 = Convex, 3 - Straight, 4 = Concave, 9 = Not Applicable
TANG_SHAPE	Number (Integer)	2	Tang Shape	0 = Indeterminate, 1 = Rounded, 2 = Lateral, 3 = Oblique, 4 = Pointed, 5 = Hanging, 9 = Not Applicable
NOTCHES	Number (Integer)	2	Notches	0 = Indeterminate, 1 = Midsection, 2 = Side, 3 = Corner, 4 = Base, 9 = Not Applicable
NOTCH_DEPTH	Number (Single)	4	Notch Depth	millimeter
SERRATED	Number (Integer)	2	Serrated	0 = Not Recorded, 1 = Heavy Serrated, 2 = Medium Serrated, 3 = Lightly Serrated, 4 = Retouched, 9 = Not Applicable
WEAR_TYPE	Number (Integer)	2	Edge Wear	0 = Indeterminate, 1 = Nibbling, 2 = Polish, 3 - Both Edges and Point, 4 = Hammering, 9 = Undocumented
WEAR_LOCATION	Number (Integer)	2	Wear Location	0 = Indeterminate, 1 = One Edge, 2 = Two Edges, 3 = Both Edges and Point, 9 = Undocumented
WEAR_SIDE	Number (Integer)	2	Wear Sides	0 = Indeterminate, 1 = One Surface, 2 = Two Surfaces, 9 = Undocumented
DRILL_ROTATION	Number (Integer)	2	Drill Rotation	0 = Indeterminate, 1 = Clockwise, 2 = Counterclockwise, 9 = Not Applicable

MATERIAL	Number (Integer)	2	Material	0 = Not Recorded, 1 = Quartzite, 2 = Argillite, 3 = Diabase, 4 = Hematite/Ochre/Limonite, 5 = Rhyolite, 6 = Gneiss, 7 = Slate/Shale, 8 = Greenstone, 9 = Schist, 10 = Metavolcanic, 11 = Chalcedony, 12 = Basalt, 13 = Quartz, 14 = Obsidian, 15 = Limestone, 16 = Diorite, 17 = Granite, 18 = Tuff, 19 = Metallic, 20 = Serpentine, 21 = Malachite, 22 = Vesicular Basalt, 23 = Cryptocrystalline Silicate, 24 = Caliche, 25 = Manganese, 26 = Calcite Crystal, 27 = Gypsum, 28 = Galena, 29 = Fossil, 30 = Epidote, 33 = Chert, 34 = Conglomerate, 35 = Jasper, 37 = Sandstone, 38 = Steatite, 39 = Amethyst, 40 = Azurite, 41 = Turquoise, 42 = Asbestos, 43 = Plagioclase Crystal, 44 = Barite Crystal, 45 = Bornite, 46 = Copper, 47 = Mica, 48 = Glass, 49 = Iron, 50 = Undocumented
LENGTH	Number (Single)	4	Length	millimeter
WIDTH	Number (Single)	4	Width	millimeter
THICKNESS	Number (Single)	4	Thickness	millimeter
WEIGHT	Number (Single)	4	Weight	gram
SPECIFIC GRAVITY	Number (Single)	4	SG	
LITHIC_COMPLETENESS	Number (Integer)	2	Completeness	0 = Incomplete, 1 = Complete
CATALOG	Number (Integer)	2	Count	
COMMENT	VARCHAR	100	Text	Words

Data Integrity

Data integrity means, in part, that you can correctly and consistently navigate and manipulate the tables in the database. There are two basic rules to ensure data integrity; entity integrity and referential integrity.

The entity integrity rule states that the value of the primary key can never be a null value (a null value is one that has no value and is not the same as a blank). Because a primary key is used to identify a unique row in a relational table, its value must always be specified and should never be unknown. The integrity rule requires that insert, update, and delete operations maintain the uniqueness and existence of all primary keys.

The referential integrity rule states that if a relational table has a foreign key, then every value of the foreign key must either be null or match the values in the relational table in which that foreign key is a primary key.

Data Integrity Rules

Data integrity is one of the cornerstones of the relational model. Simply stated data integrity means that the data values in the database are correct and consistent.

Data integrity is enforced in the relational model by entity and referential integrity rules. Although not part of the relational model, most database software enforce attribute integrity through the use of domain information.

Entity Integrity

The entity integrity rule states that for every instance of an entity, the value of the primary key must exist, be unique, and cannot be null. Without entity integrity, the primary key could not fulfill its role of uniquely identifying each instance of an entity.

Referential Integrity

The referential integrity rule states that every foreign key value must match a primary key value in an associated table. Referential integrity ensures that we can correctly navigate between related entities.

Insert and Delete Rules

A foreign key creates a hierarchical relationship between two associated entities. The entity containing the foreign key is the child, or dependent, and the table containing the primary key from which the foreign key values are obtained is the parent.

In order to maintain referential integrity between the parent and child as data is inserted or deleted from the database certain insert and delete rules must be considered.

Insert Rules

Insert rules commonly implemented are:

- Dependent. The dependent insert rule permits insertion of child entity instance only if matching parent entity already exists.
- Automatic. The automatic insert rule always permits insertion of child entity instance. If matching parent entity instance does not exist, it is created.
- Nullify. The nullify insert rule always permits the insertion of child entity instance. If a matching parent entity instance does not exist, the foreign key in child is set to null.
- Default. The default insert rule always permits insertion of child entity instance. If a matching parent entity instance does not exist, the foreign key in the child is set to previously defined value.
- Customized. The customized insert rule permits the insertion of child entity instance only if certain customized validity constraints are met.
- No Effect. This rule states that the insertion of child entity instance is always permitted. No matching parent entity instance need exist, and thus no validity checking is done.

Delete Rules

- Restrict. The restrict delete rule permits deletion of parent entity instance only if there are no matching child entity instances.
- Cascade. The cascade delete rule always permits deletion of a parent entity instance and deletes all matching instances in the child entity.
- Nullify. The nullify delete rules always permits deletion of a parent entity instance. If any matching child entity instances exist, the values of the foreign keys in those instances are set to null.
- Default. The default rule always permits deletion of a parent entity instance. If any matching child entity instances exist, the value of the foreign keys are set to a predefined default value.
- Customized. The customized delete rule permits deletion of a parent entity instance only if certain validity constraints are met.
- No Effect. The no effect delete rule always permits deletion of a parent entity instance. No validity checking is done.

Delete and Insert Guidelines

The choice of which rule to use is determined by some basic guidelines for insert and delete rules are given below.

- Avoid use of nullify insert or delete rules. Generally, the parent entity in a parent-child relationship has mandatory existence. Use of the null insert or delete rule would violate this rule.
- Use either automatic or dependent insert rule for generalization hierarchies. Only these rules will keep the rule that all instances in the subtypes must also be in the supertype.
- Use the cascade delete rule for generalization hierarchies. This rule will enforce the rule that only instances in the supertype can appear in the subtypes.

Domains

A domain is a valid set of values for an attribute which enforce that values from an insert or update make sense. Each attribute in the model should be assigned domain information which includes:

- Data Type—Basic data types are integer, decimal, or character. Most data bases support variants of these plus special data types for date and time.
- Length—This is the number of digits or characters in the value. For example, a value of 5 digits or 40 characters.
- Date Format—The format for date values such as dd/mm/yy or yy/mm/dd
- Range—The range specifies the lower and upper boundaries of the values the attribute may legally have

- Constraints—Are special restrictions on allowable values. For example, the Beginning_Pay_Date for a new employee must always be the first work day of the month of hire.
- Null support—Indicates whether the attribute can have null values
- Default value (if any)—The value an attribute instance will have if a value is not entered.

Primary Key Domains

The values of primary keys must be unique and nulls are not allowed.

Foreign Key Domains

The data type, length, and format of primary keys must be the same as the corresponding primary key. The uniqueness property must be consistent with relationship type. A one-to-one relationship implies a unique foreign key; a one-to-many relationship implies a non-unique foreign key.

Relational Databases versus Database Servers

Not all databases are relational, and not all relational databases are built on the client/server paradigm. But most of the time the survey will want a relational database server, so it is important to clarify the distinction.

Remember: a relational database manipulates only tables and the result of all operations are also tables. The tables are sets, which are themselves sets of rows and columns. The view of the database is itself a set of tables.

Also, a DBF file is not a relational database. A DBF table is not manipulated as a set (you are always following an index), and you do not perform operations on tables that yield other tables as the result (you are just looping through records from one or more tables, even when you use the "SET RELATION" dBase statement).

Most database file formats are not relational databases. Even the BTrieve server NLM is *not* a relational database, because you do not operate on sets tables or sets of tables.

Conversely, a MDB file (from MS Access) is a relational database. Although you can open and manipulate a MDB file just like a DBF file, navigating through records and index, you can also perform all operations through a relational view of the database and using SQL statements. This is why Access is an ideal database manager for a survey.

Actually, most nonrelational databases are based on some "navigational" model: a hierarchy, a linked list, a B-Tree, etc. It is common to refer to these as ISAM (Indexed Sequential Access Method) Databases.

Now let us see what is a database server: it is a specialized process that manages the database itself. The applications are clients to the database server, and they never manipulate the database directly, but only make requests for the server to perform these operations.

This allows the server to add many sophisticated features, such as transaction processing, recovery, backup, access control, etc. without increasing the complexity of every application. The server also reduces the risk of data file corruption, if only because only the server writes to the database (a crash on any client machine will not leave unflushed buffers).

A general database server also takes advantage of the client/server architecture to lower network usage. If you open a DBF or MDB file stored on a file server, you need to retrieve every record just to filter out which ones you really need. But if you connect to a database server, it filters out the unneeded records and sends to the client only the data that really matters.

Access is a relational database, but it is not a database server. mSQL, SQL Anywhere, DB2, Oracle are both relational databases and database servers. The Btrieve NLM is a database server, but it is not a relational database.

Appendix E – The McCary Survey Recording Form

The following form is used by the McCary Survey to record fluted points. Readers are invited to use it or create a similar form based on their research and recording needs.

McCary Survey® Record Form				
Record Date:	**Recorder:**	**Location:**	**Finder:**	**Owner:**
Find Type:	**Discovery Date:**	**County:**	**River:**	**Artifact Number:**
Site: Yes: _____ No: _____ VA Number: _____ 44 _____	**Condition:** Complete: _____ Broken: _____ Damaged: _____ Rechip: _____	**Manufacture:** Biface: _____ Uniface: _____ Tool: _____	**Basic Shape:** Lanceolate: _____ Triangular: _____ Pentagonal: _____ Other: _____	Flakes/cm Face #1 _____ Face #2 _____ Average: _____
Length: _____ mm **Width:** _____mm **Thick:** _____mm **C to C:** _____ mm **Tip:** _____ °	**Material:** Grain: Source: **Weight:** _____ grams **Specific Gravity:**_____	**Color:** **Munsell:** **Record Temp:** _____ °	**Face #1 Flute:** Single: _____ Multiple: ____ Width: _____ mm Height: _____mm Type: _____ Ending: _____	**Face #2 Flute:** Single: _____ Multiple: ____ Width: _____ mm Height: _____mm Type: _____ Ending: _____
Bevel: _____ **Face(s):** _____	**Flaking Quality:** Hinges:	**Serrations:** Retouch:	**Cross Section:**	**Lateral Thinning:**
Blade, Left: Straight:____ Incurve: ____ Excurve: ____	**Blade, Right:** Straight:____ Incurve: ____ Excurve: ____	**Concavity:** Width: _____mm Height: _____mm Ground: _____	**Grinding:** Stem:_____ Base: _____ Degree: _____	**D/P** Tip: _____ mm Base: _____mm
Photo Nrs: Film: _____ Digital: _____	**Rubbings:** Made: _____ Both Faces: _____	**Drawings:** Made: _____ Both Faces: _____	**Water Sample:** Nr: _____ pH: _____	**Heat Treatment:** Yes: _____ No: _____
General Observations:			**Map Attached: Yes ____, No ____** **Discovery witness: Yes ___, No ___**	
Owner address: **City, State, Zip** **Phone:** **Email:**				

Appendix F – Gifts

DEED OF GIFT

Whereas, the [individual or name of agency], hereafter called the Donor, hereby deeds title of the artifacts listed in Attachment A to the public domain as provided in this Deed;

Whereas, the [name of the individual, state/federal agency, society, or public institution], hereinafter called the Recipient, is dedicated to the preservation and protection of artifacts, specimens and associated records that are generated in connection with its activities, projects, and programs;

And furthermore, the Recipient maintains a public policy with all archaeological investigations and acquisitions; And, acts as a public domain for these artifacts and associated materials and records;

Whereas, certain artifacts and specimens, listed in Attachment A to this Deed of Gift, were recovered from lands where the donor had rights to investigate with the donor's interest in obtaining prehistoric Native American artifacts;

And furthermore, the Donor has free and clear title and possession to these artifacts;

Whereas, the Donor is desirous of donating the artifacts and specimens to the Recipient to ensure their continued preservation, curation, and protection;

Whereas, the Recipient hereby gratefully acknowledges the receipt of the artifacts and specimens and will retain these artifacts and specimens in the public domain and make them available for scientific research; and

Now therefore, the Donor does hereby unconditionally donate to the Recipient, for unrestricted use, title to the artifacts and specimens listed in Attachment A to this Deed of Gift.

Signed [signature of the Donor]

Date: [date]

Signed: [signature of the Recipient]

Date: [date]

Attachment A: Inventory of Artifacts and Specimens or attached documents on these artifacts.

Appendix G – Point Rubbings and Drawings

For more than a hundred years, rubbings and drawings have been the principal way to record projectile points. While digital photography has generally replaced these techniques, they still remain the best way to portray details and actual properties in morphology. The following provides an overview of these techniques (Figure G1). Hranicky and Johnson (2005) provide details in recording paleopoints.

Rubbings

To record a point's face, soft paper is placed on the point's surface. By rubbing the finger over the surface, the flake scar ridges push up into the paper leaving an impression. Next, use a soft lead pencil or charcoal square to lightly rub over the raised flake scars. After completion, make a Xerox copy or coat the drawing with a lacquer. The rubbing can be used to make drawings, also.

Drawings

To record a point's surface, the point is placed under a magnifying lens next to drawing paper. Using a pencil, the outline of the point is drawn first. Next, start at the distal end and sketch down the medial axis. Then, work outward. After the pencil drawing is completed, ink the drawing. A scale is usually drawn, also.

Photo Sketching

Another technique is to photograph the point using a digital camera. Then print out the point on a large format (8 ½ x 11 in) paper. Next, place the printout on a light table and trace the flake scars.

G1 – Point Rubbing and Drawing Examples

Rubbings:

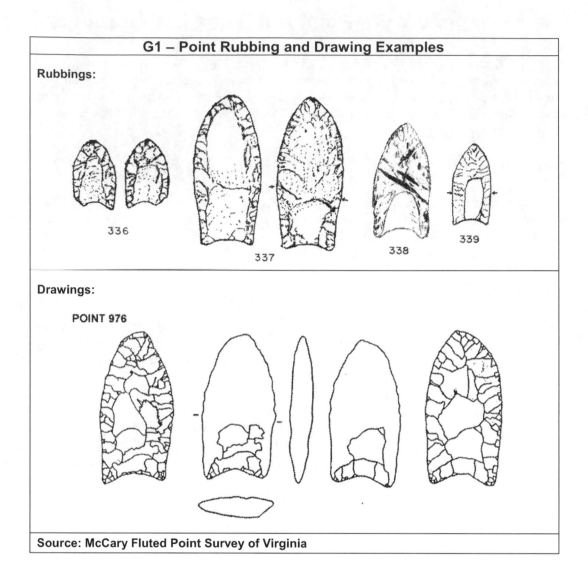

Drawings:

POINT 976

Source: McCary Fluted Point Survey of Virginia

APPENDIX H - ARCHAEOLOGICAL RECORDS

All documentation, paper or magnetic, pertaining to artifacts and sites must be maintained by state and federal agencies forever. Storage can be any form and location; however, records are public and must be available to anyone with appropriate needs to examine them. According to the Code of Federal Regulations as Part 79 of Title 36:

Associated records means original records (or copies thereof) that are prepared, assembled and document efforts to locate, evaluate, record, study, preserve or recover a prehistoric or historic resource. Some records such as field notes, artifact inventories and oral histories may be originals that are prepared as a result of the field work, analysis and report preparation. Other records such as deeds, survey plats, historical maps and diaries may be copies of original public or archival documents that are assembled and studies as a result of historical research. Classes of associated records (and illustrative examples) that may be in a collection include, but are not limited to:

(I) Records relating to the identification, evaluation, documentation, study, preservation or recovery of a resource (such as site forms, field notes, drawings, maps, photographs, slides, negatives, films, video and audio cassette tapes, oral histories, artifact inventories, laboratory reports, computer cards and tapes, computer disks and diskettes, printouts of computerized data, manuscripts, reports, and accession, catalog and inventory records);

(ii) Records relating to the identification of a resource using remote sensing methods and equipment (such as satellite and serial photography and imagery, side scan sonar, magnetometers, subbottom profilers, radar and fathometers);

(iii) Public records essential to understanding the resource (such as deeds, survey plats, military and census records, birth, marriage and death certificates, immigration and naturalization papers, tax forms and reports);

(iv) Archival records essential to understanding the resource (such as historical maps, drawings and photographs, manuscripts, architectural and landscape plans, correspondence, diaries, ledgers, catalogs and receipts); and

(v) Administrative records relating to the survey, excavation or other study of the resource (such as scopes of work, requests for proposals, research proposals, contracts, antiquities permits, reports, documents relating to compliance with section 106 of the National Historic Preservation Act (16 U.S.C. 470f), and National Register of Historic Places nomination and determination of eligibility forms).

APPENDIX I – PARTS OF A PROJECTILE POINT

Numerous publications for projectile point identification are available. As an example, see Hranicky (2004)

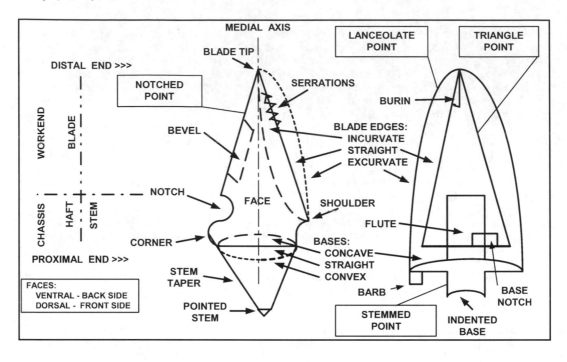

APPENDIX J – SKILL IN TOOLMAKING

Skill - proficiency, talent, ability, and dexterity to produce lithic tools; all of which can be called an artist or craftsman (Hranicky 2004). For lithic technology, it requires specialized ability, training, and experience. Also, it requires skill levels which constitute knapper's ability and competency to replicate tools that meet social norms. Normal tools always reflect high skill levels. Change occurs when variation in tool styles occurs at high levels of skill. If a new style is not considered as a high level of skill (evaluation) by the social unit, then it is a knapping mistake or failure. According to Coe (1975):

The worker must either modify or develop techniques which conform and respond to the material being used -- a fact that seems to be frequently overlooked by archaeologists.

For most high-quality flint implements, such as the Duck River Cache of Tennessee, high-level skill is assumed by most archaeologists. Even among other professional disciplines, the study and classification of skill did not receive much attention until the 1940s (see Bartlett 1943). Furthermore, the definition of skill and defining basic elements are also lacking, especially in archaeology. Welford (1976) argues that all skills involve:

1 – Perceptual skill - giving coherence to the sensory data received through the sense organs and storing it in memory for future use. This skill has a wide range of ability in humans. Training in this skill is necessary for archaeology, such as recognizing any given point in a wide range of point types.

2 – Intellectual skill - ability to create combinations of activities to create new events, objects, or goals. Decision making based on memory to produce a desired or expected outcome of an activity.

3 – Movement control skill - ability to perform specific physical activities. Generally, well-practiced movements are noted for their lack of intellectual control. This skill generally involves spatial and temporal factors, such as hunting deer with a bow and arrow.

Skill levels in flintknapping:

1 – Master level - knapper who has the skill to make high quality ceremonial flaked implements. An example of flaking is ribbon flaking on a projectile point.

2 – Expert - skill that is required to make, thin, well-shaped points. An example is the fluted Clovis point.

3 – Craftsman 1 - average skill that produces moderate quality points, such as the Adena point. Points have careful and fine flaking patterns.

4 – Craftsman 2 - skill to make consistent points out of numerous materials. Examples are Morrow Mountain and Savannah River points. Points have a random flaking pattern and are usually thick points.

5 – Novice - crudely-shaped points indicative of learning knapping or someone who will never learn the craft.

Skill Test for an **expert** flintknapper is:

1 – Implement requirements: make a biface 350 mm long, 50 mm wide and 6 mm thick

2 – Knapping requirements: biface shall be flat with no medial ridge; width will be 6 mm anywhere on the biface

3 – Material requirements: fine-grain flint with no impurities

4 – Time constraints: none, but within several hours

5 – Billet: choice of the knapper

6 – Flaker: choice of the knapper

7 – Bulb-scar remains - bulb cannot exceed the thickness of the biface

8 – Platform (port) - must remain to show spall preparation

9 – Edges - uniform with no edge indentations..

To perform this test, the knapper must have considerable practice making the necessary controlled movements in knapping. This is an intellectual dominated activity in which the knapper must know every detail and methods to accomplish the task, such as the decisions for solving each stage of manufacture. The knapper can make errors but should have skill to overcome them. Most experts are not going to make mistakes, but material failure happens to all knappers. Skilled performance is almost exclusively automatic for the knapper.

Caution is needed to assign skill levels to prehistoric tools or toolkits, because:

1 – No way to determine the learning curve

2 – No way to measure practice hours in tool production

3 – No way to adjust to different lithic material

4 – No way to classify skill by time periods

5 – No way to classify skill by acceptable social levels

6 – No way to determine skill by geography

Cognitive behavior is manifested in varying degrees of skill. The best is an average of skill over various times and places, all of which are based on contemporary scientific analyses. Additionally, performance based on skill can be observed in archaeological contexts. The inference here is high-quality implements assume a high level of skill. This is observable on flaked implements as:

1 – Fineness of flaking
2 – Adherence to cultural style
3 – High-quality material.

Skill should not be confused with cognitive process or abilities if it is only used as some type IQ measurement. Physically ability to perform a task varies among individuals, because some people can accomplish one or more of the following (intelligences):

1 – Language task - orators, speechmaking, etc.
2 – Logic/mathematics - formulation, reason, etc.
3 – Music - song, dance, etc.
4 – Spacial - time, distance, migration, etc.
5 – Bodily - manual, task performance, etc.
6 – Personal (intra) – people relationships, etc.
7 – Personal (inter) - inner spirit, future, etc.

For lithic technology, we are concerned with numbers 2 and 5. Fortunately, these two factors are directly observable in the archaeological record. Skill involves physical ability to perform successfully a given task. However, unless the skill is performed in a social setting, it does not exist because it is evaluated as a skill by the culture; it is a value judgment. For toolmaking, skill can be considered as levels or stages in a production process. These levels are:

1 – Process capability or procurement of needed resources

2 – Knowledge capability as needed for manufacture

3 – Institutional capability as needed to implement tools into a society

4 – Infrastructure capability needed to use tools in a cultural unit or setting

5 – Adequate physical motor control of muscles

6 – Ability to use space and it dimensions appropriately (culturally determined space utilization).

Various skills are needed in the tool life cycle. Once the tool is expended, the process starts all over again. All skills meet two basic needs:

1 – Social needs
2 – Physical needs.

Skill involves a refined (disciplined) motor pattern, which is a high-level mental process of the brain. The term orchestrating (see Baron 1987) denotes a physical movement of translating the motor pattern and applying it. Application involves the cerebellum, spinal reflex circuits, motor neurons, and muscles. Planning is a mental process of recalling or generating motor patterns and uniting the necessary physical apparatus into a complex movement. Memory is associated which stores the correct application pattern as parameters. Parameters include, but are not limited to:

1 – Intended speed
2 – Intended spatial size or dimension
3 – Expected forces.

In knapping, for example, the intended size regulates the size of the knapp-object. Knapping is primarily done with finger and hand movements. However, depending on force, the arm, shoulder, and torso become factors for working large pieces or quarrying. For skill,

1 – Motor pattern is modified as a function of the correct force

2 – Recalling correct factors, such as speed, force, and position.

Skill involves learning and experience of young people through the elderly. Skill learning occurs as:

1 – Cognitive stage - description of the toolmaking procedure is learned.

2 – Associative stage - personal method(s) for performing the skill is worked out; this may not be possible with all individuals. Thus, ability is a factor.

3 – Autonomous stage - skill becomes more and more rapid and automatic.

Skill can be measured if the research assumes accurate and rapid tool production is the principal concern of skill. A scale, such as Blackburn's (1936) power law of practice, is used to measure required time over required accuracy, which is:

$$\zeta \, \text{Skill} = \log (T)/(\log (A)/M^{-x})$$

whereas:
    T = time
    A = accuracy
    M = memory
    ζ = definable skill or function

Note: Logarithms are not needed; they are the preference of the author.

For analysis, additional factors K (knapper), F (functor), and S (structor) can be used for specific tools (in: Hranicky 2004). Testing this process requires a computer simulation program where these variables can be adjusted. Knapping measurements are a long way from any scientific usage, but the possibility offers an endless study of the prehistoric flintknapper.

Finally, skill can be considered as individualistic or collective skills in a group. These skills may be manifested in the archaeological context, such as specific flaking patterns, materials, platforms, shapes, styles, etc. Skill levels must be observed on paleopoints in order to determine their classification.

Chart J1 - Skill and Technology Levels

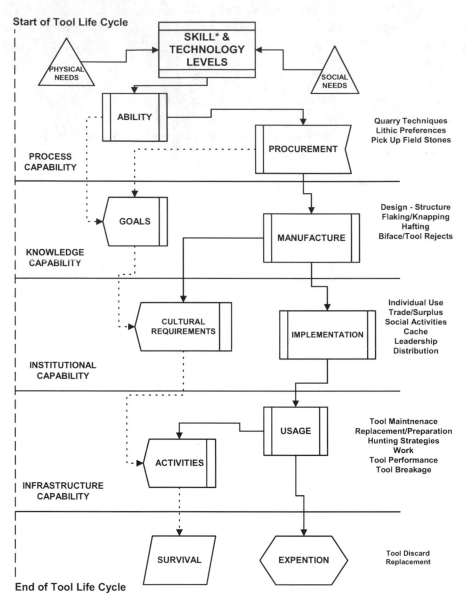

Start of Tool Life Cycle

PHYSICAL NEEDS

SKILL* & TECHNOLOGY LEVELS

SOCIAL NEEDS

ABILITY

PROCUREMENT — Quarry Techniques / Lithic Preferences / Pick Up Field Stones

PROCESS CAPABILITY

GOALS

MANUFACTURE — Design - Structure / Flaking/Knapping / Hafting / Biface/Tool Rejects

KNOWLEDGE CAPABILITY

CULTURAL REQUIREMENTS

IMPLEMENTATION — Individual Use / Trade/Surplus / Social Activities / Cache / Leadership / Distribution

INSTITUTIONAL CAPABILITY

USAGE — Tool Maintnenace / Replacement/Preparation / Hunting Strategies / Work / Tool Performance / Tool Breakage

ACTIVITIES

INFRASTRUCTURE CAPABILITY

SURVIVAL

EXPENTION — Tool Discard / Replacement

End of Tool Life Cycle

* = Individual and Group Skills

132

References

Angel, Edward
(2002) Interactive Computer Graphics. Addicon-Wesley, Reading, MA.

Aukstakalis S. and D. Blatner
(1992) Silicon Mirage: The Art and Science of Virtual Reality. Peachpit Press, Inc., Berkeley, CA.

Baron, Robert J.
(1987) The Cerebral Computer - An Introduction to the Computational Structure of the Human Brain. Lawrence Erlbaum Associates, Publishers, Hillsdale, NJ.

Benthall, Joseph L. and Ben C. McCary
(1973) The Williamson Site: A New Approach. Archaeology of Eastern North America, Vol. 1, No. 1, pp. 127-132.

Blackburn, J. M.
(1936) Acquisition of Skill: An Analysis of Learning Curves. IHRB Report No. 73.

Bladock, H. M..
(1972) Social Statistics. McGraw-Hill, Inc., New York, NY.

Brennan, Louis A.
(1982) A Compilation of Fluted Points of Eastern North America by Count and Distribution: An ANEA Project. Archaeology of Eastern North America, Vol. 10, pp. 27-46.

Carroll, Mary S.
(2002) Delivering Archaeological Information Electronically. Society for American Archaeology, Washington, DC.

Clarke, David L.
(1968) Analytical Archaeology. Methuern, London.

Connolly, Thomas M. and Carolyn E. Begg
(2005) Database Systems: A Practical Approach to Design, Implementation, and Management. Addison-Wesley, Boston, MA.

Demolomber, R.
(1997) Answering Queries about Validity and Completeness of Data: from Model Logic to Relational Algerbre. In: T. Andreasen, H. Christiansen, and H. Larson, editors, Flexible Quary Answering Systems. Kluwer Academic Publishers, New York, NY.
(1996) Validity Queries and Completeness Queries. In: Proceedings of the 9th International Symposium on Methodologies for Intelligent Systems.

Egloff, Keith T. and Joseph M. McAvoy
(1998) A Tribute to Ben C. McCary. ASV Quarterly Bulletin, Vol. 53, No. 4, pp. 138-148.

Fleming, Canace C. and Barbara von Halle
(1989) Handbook of Relational Database Design. Addison Wesley, New York, NY.

Foley, J. D. and A. van Dam, et al.
(1990) Computer Graphics: Principles and Practice. Addison-Wesley, Reading, MA.

Hatch, Allen
(2002) Algerbric Topology. Cambridge University Press, New York, NY.

Hoard, Robert J., William E. Banks, Rolfe D. Mandel, Michael Finnegan, and Jennifer E. Epperson
(2004) A Middle Archaic From East Central Kansas. American Antiquity, Vol. 69, No. 4, pp. 717-739.

Holmes, William H.
(1897) Stone Implements of the Potomac-Chesapeake Tidewater Province. Bureau of American Ethnology Annual Report, 1893-94, pp. 13-152.

Howard, Edgar B.
(1943) Evidence of Early Man in North America. Museum Journal, Publications of the University Museums of Pennsylvania, Vol. 24, Nos. 2-3, p.107.

Hranicky, Wm Jack
(2004) An Encyclopedia of Concepts and Terminology in American Prehistoric Lithic Technology. AuthorHouse, Bloomington, IN.
(2003a) Projectile Point Typology Along the Atlantic Coastal Plain. Universal Publishers, uPublish.com, FL.
(2003b) Terminology and Nomenclature for American Projectile Points. Virginia Academic Press, Alexandria, VA.
(2003c) Analytical Concepts for American Indian Tools. Virginia Academic Press, Alexandria, VA.
(1989) The McCary Survey of Virginia Fluted Points: An Example of Collector Involvement in Virginia Archeology. ASV Quarterly Bulletin, Vol. 44, No. 1, pp. 20-24.

Hranicky, Wm Jack and Ben C. McCary
(1996) Clovis Technology in Virginia. Archeological Society of Virginia Special Publication Number 31.

Hranicky, Wm Jack and Floyd Painter
(1989) A Guide to the Identification of Virginia Projectile Points. Archeological Society of Virginia Special Publication Number 17.

Hranicky, Wm Jack and Michael F. Johnson
(2005) Recording Clovis Points – Techniques, Examples, and Methods. To be published …

Jameson, J. H.
(1997) Presenting Archaeology to the Public. AltaMira Press, Walnut Groove, CA.

Justice, Noel D.
(1987) Stone Age Spear Points of the Midcontinental and Eastern United States. Indiana University Press, Bloomington, IN.

Kantardzic, Mehmed
(2003) Data Mining – Concepts, Models, Methods, and Algorithms. Wiley-Interscience, New York, NY.

Kifer, Michael, Arthur Bernstein, and Philip Lewis
(2005) Database Systems: An Application-Oriented Approach, Introductory Version (2nd edition). Addison-Wesley, Boston, MA.

King, Mary Elizabeth
(1980) Curators: Ethics and Obligations. Curator, Vol. 23, No. 1, pp. 10-18.

Klecka, William R.
(1980) Discriminant Analysis. Quantitative Applications in the Social Sciences Series, No. 19. Sage Publications, Thousand Oaks, CA.

Kraft, C. Herbert
(1973) The Plenge Site: A Paleo-Indian Occupation Site in New Jersey. Archaeology of Eastern North America, Vol. 1, No. 1, pp. 56-117.

Krieger, Alex D.
(1944) The Typological Concept. American Antiquity, Vol. 9, pp. 271-288.

Larson, J. A.
(1995) Database Directions: From Relational to Distributed, Multimedia and Object-Oriented Systems. Prentice Hall, Upper Saddle River, NJ.

Lattanzi, Gregory
(1999) Cultural Resource Management and the Internet: A Touch of "Gray." SAA Bulletin, Vol. 17, No. 4, pp. 30-33.

Link, Edward P.
(2000) An Audit of the System, Not of the People. Quality Pursuit, Inc., Rocherster, NY.

Lock, Andrew and Charles R. Peters, eds.
(1996) Handbook of Human Symbolic Evolution. Clarendon Press, Oxford.

Mason, Ronald J.
(1962) The Paleo-Indian Tradition in Eastern North America. Current Anthropology, Vol. 3, No. 3, pp. 227-84.

McCary, Ben C.
(1975) The Williamson Paleoindian Site, Dinwiddie County, Virginia. Chesopiean, Vol. 13, pp. 48-131.
(1951) A Workshop Site of Early Man, Dinwiddie County, Virginia. American Antiquity, Vol. 17, pp. 9-17.

McFadden, F. R., J. A. Hoffer, and M. B. Prescott
(1999) Modern Database Management. Addison-Wesley, Reading, MA.

McGimsey III, Charles R.
(1972) Public Archaeology. Seminar Press, New York, NY.

Perino, Gregory
(1991) Selected Preforms, Points, and Knives of the North American Indians, Vol. 2, Points and Barbs Press, Idabel, OK
(1985) Selected Preforms, Points, and Knives of the North American Indians, Vol. 1, Points and Barbs Press, Idabel, OK.

Roberts, Frank H. H. Jr.
(1938) The Folsom Problem in American Archeology. Smithsonian Report for 1938, p. 543.

Sullivan, Lynne P. and S. Terry Childs
(2003) Curating Archaeological Collections. Archaeologist Toolkit 6, Altamira Press, Walnut Creek, CA.

Tabachnick, Barbara G. and Linda S. Fidell
(2001) Using Multivariate Statistics. Allyn and Bacon Publishers, Boston, MA.

Tankersley, Kenneth
(2002) In Search of Ice Age Americans. Gilbert Smith Publishers, Salt Lake City, UT.

Terrell, John
(1979) What is a Curator? Field Museum Bulletin, Vol. 50, No. 4, pp. 16-17.

Turban, Efraim and Jay E. Aronson
(2001) Decision Support System and Intelligent Systems. Prentice Hall, Upper Saddle River, NJ.

Wormington, Hannah Marie
(1966) The Spirit of Worthwhile Collecting. Chesopiean, Vol. 4, Nos. 4-5, pp. 134-36.
(1962) A Survey of Early American Prehistory. American Scientist, Vol. 50, No. 1, pp. 230-242.
(1957) Ancient Man in North America. Denver Museum of Natural History Popular Series, No. 4, 4th edition.

Printed in the United States
by Baker & Taylor Publisher Services